GAYLE'S MAJESTIC ARTWORKS

www.gaylesepicartworks.com

By Gayle L. Daufel

Copyright © 2023 by Gayle L. Daufel

ISBN: 978-1-77883-004-4 (Paperback)

The views expressed in this book are solely those of the author and do not necessarily reflect the views of the publisher, and the publisher hereby disclaims any responsibility for them.

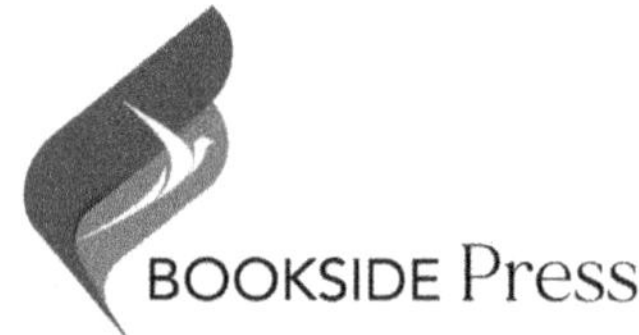

BookSide Press
877-741-8091
www.booksidepress.com
orders@booksidepress.com

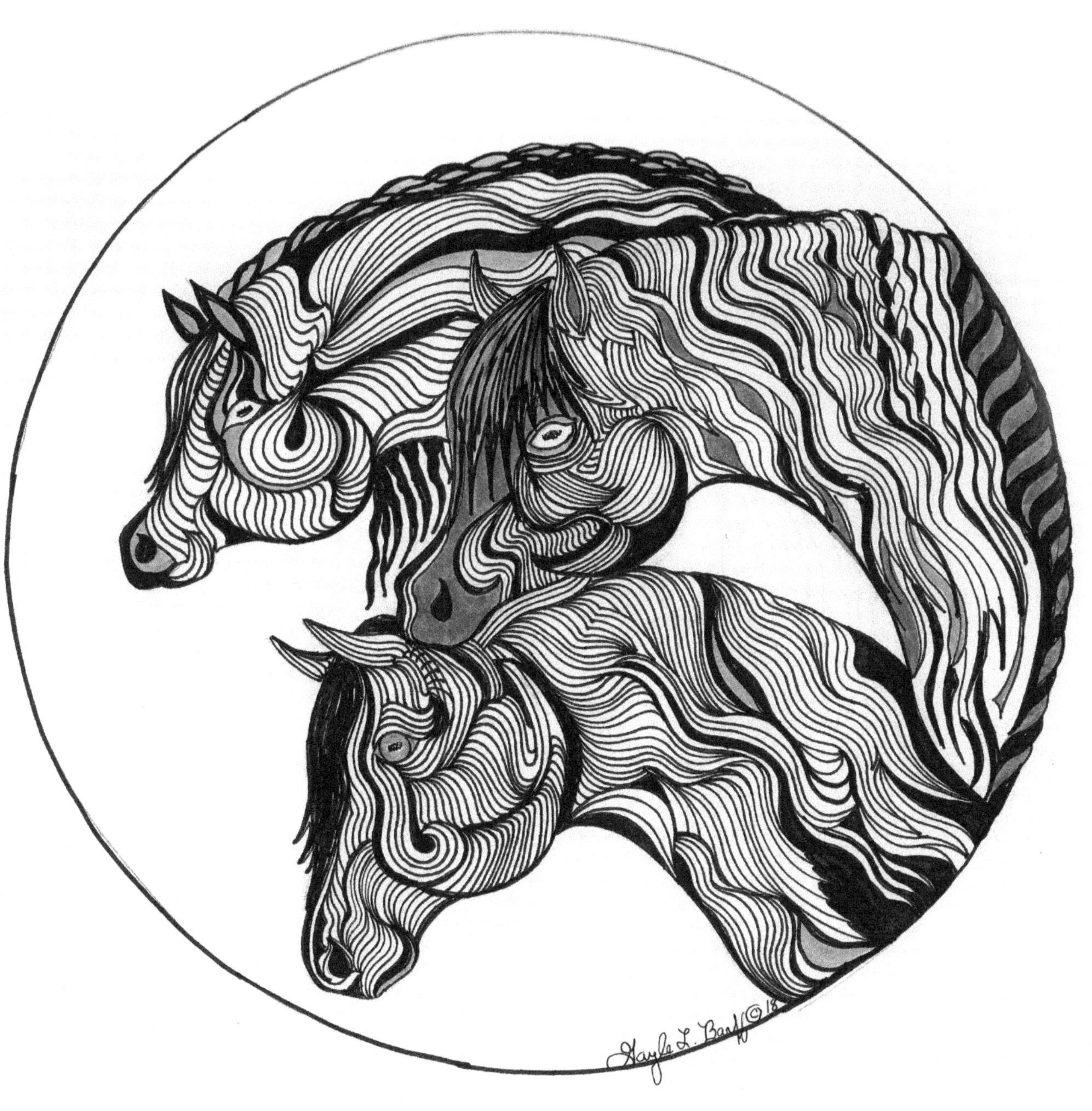

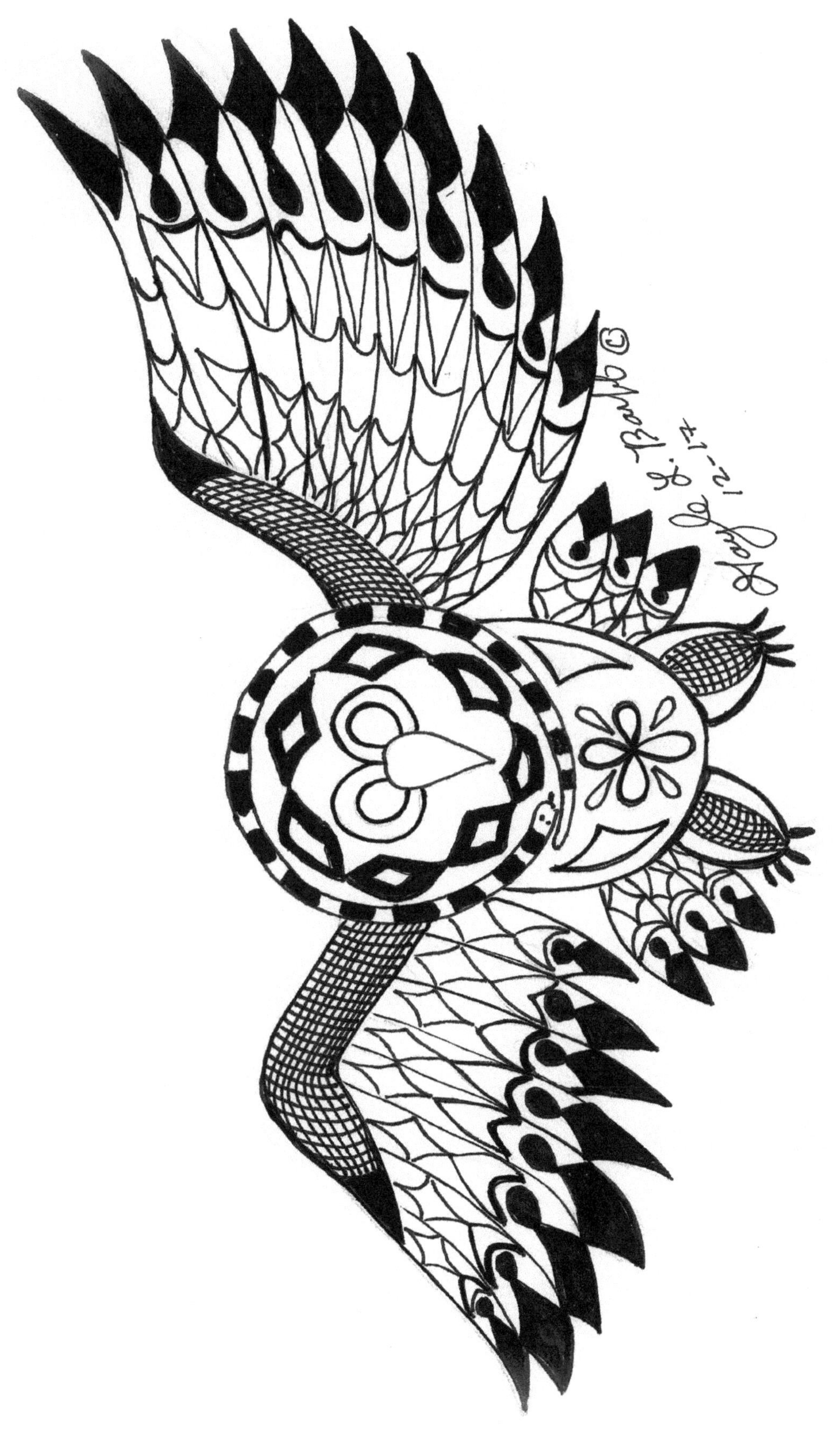

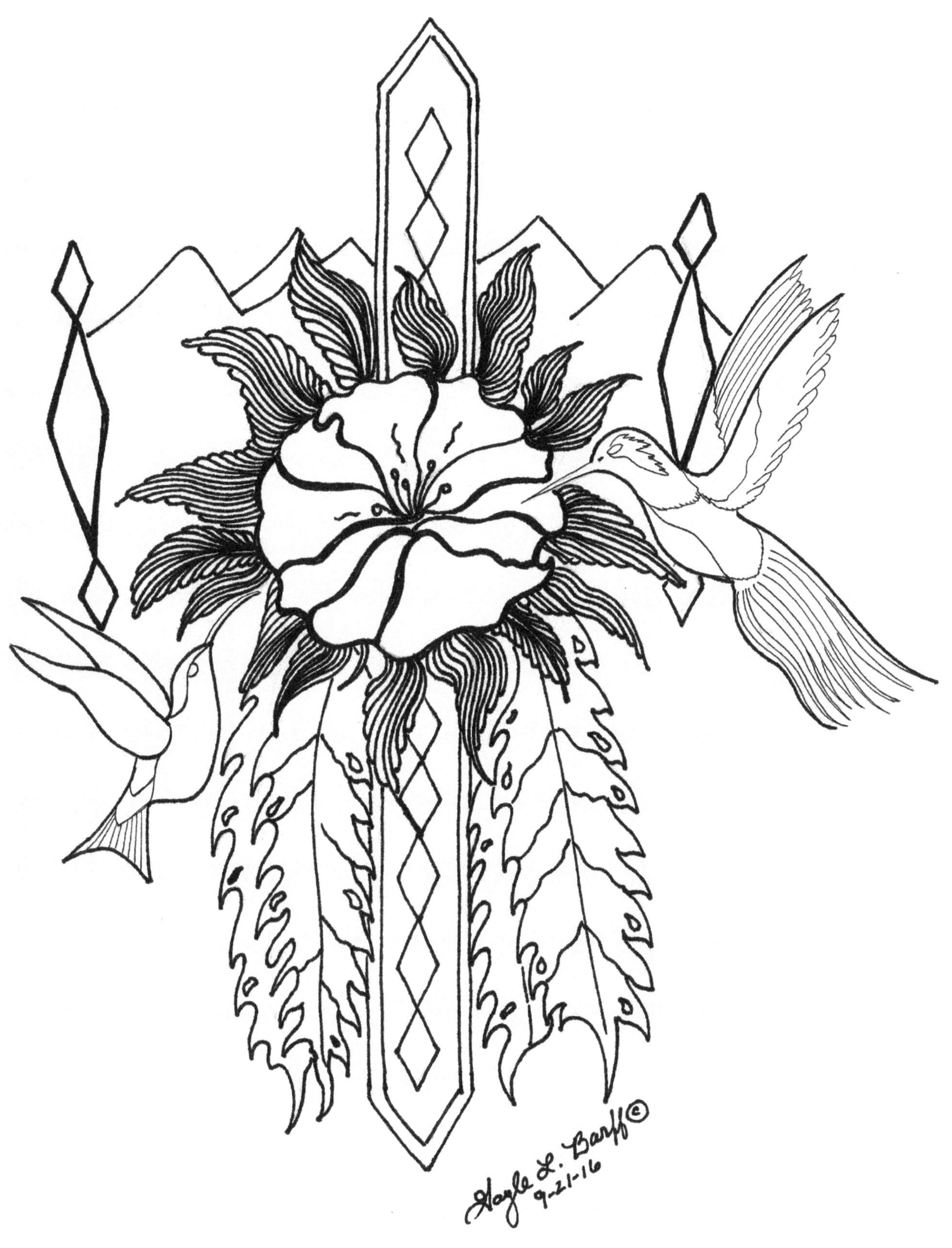

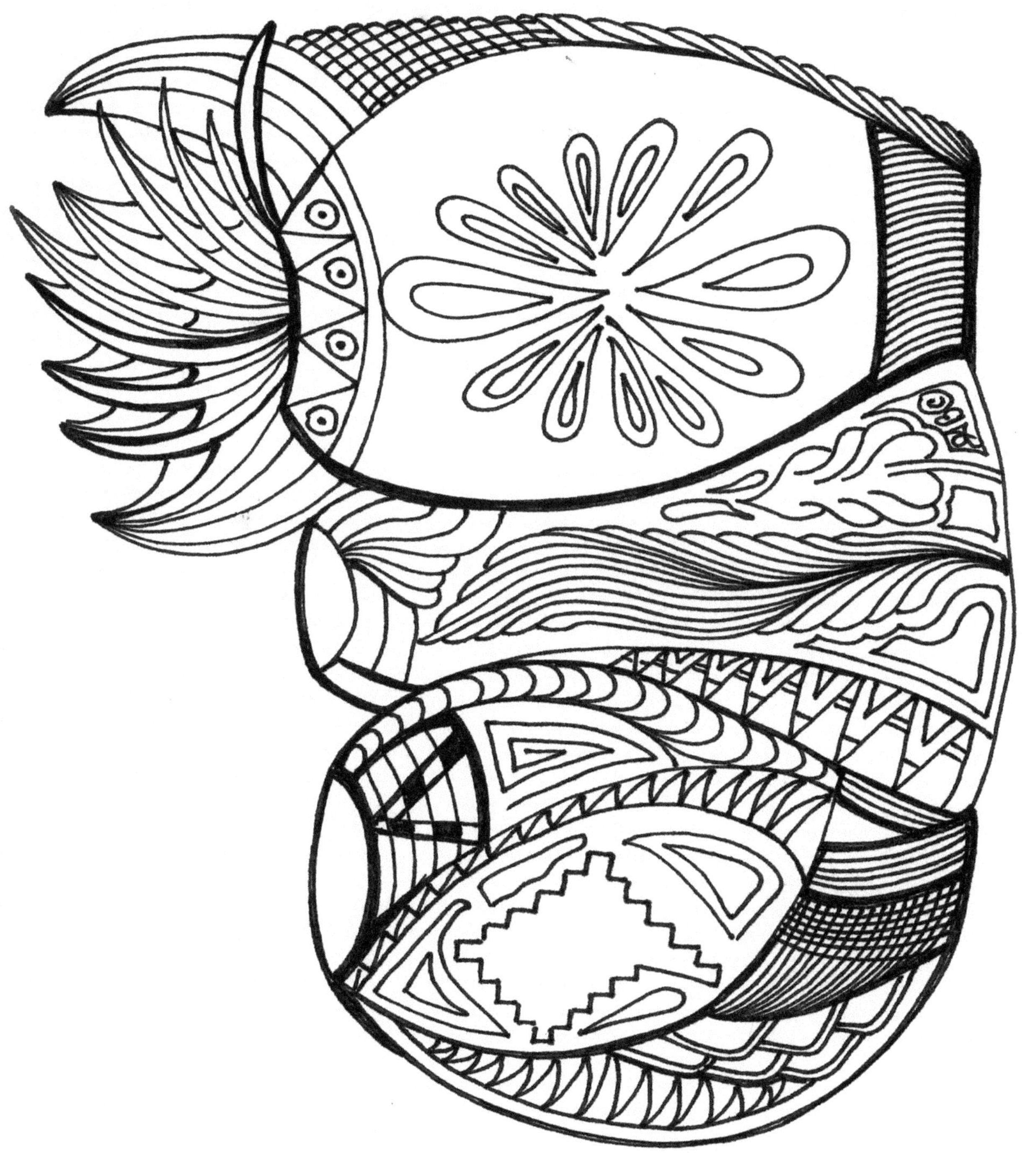

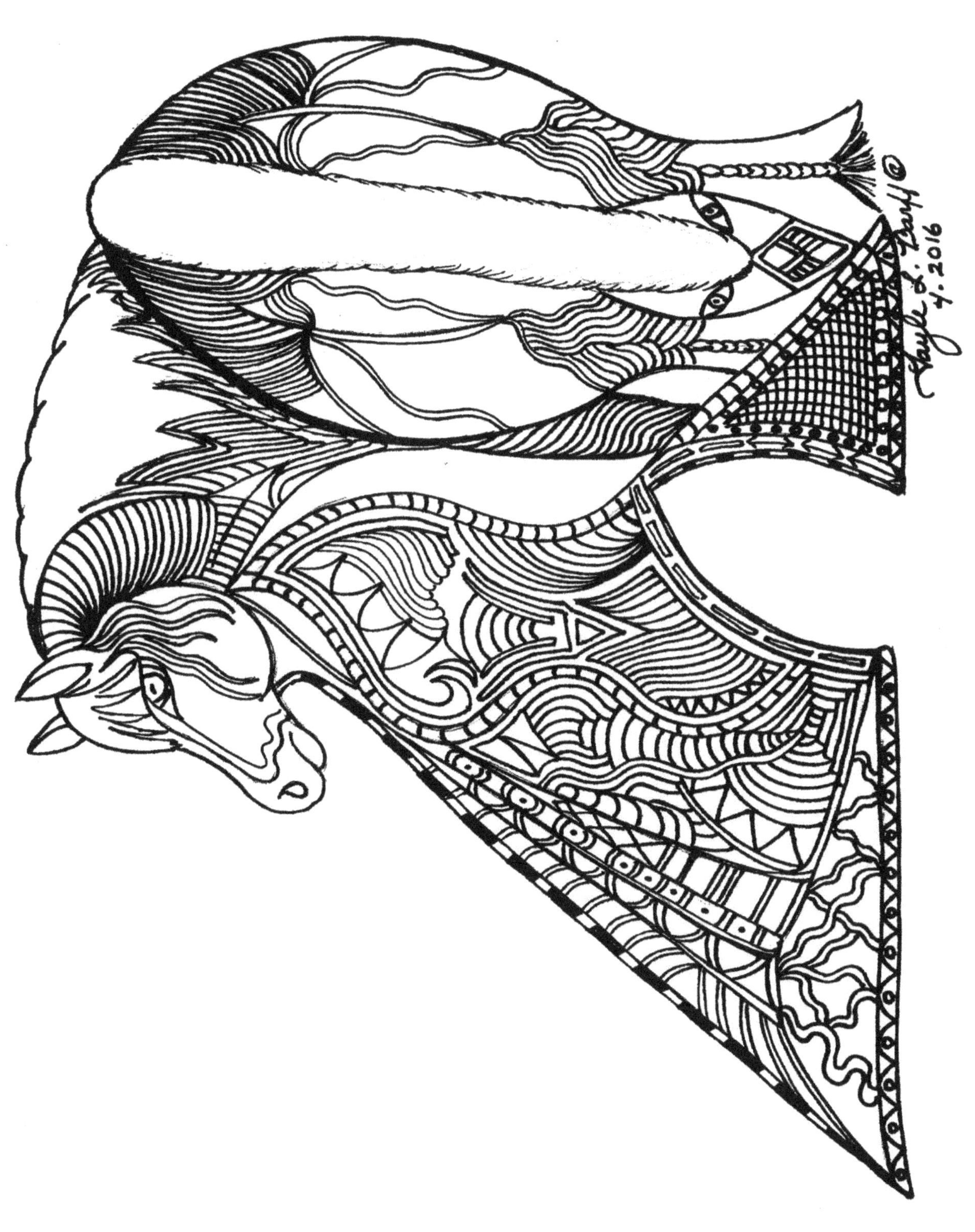

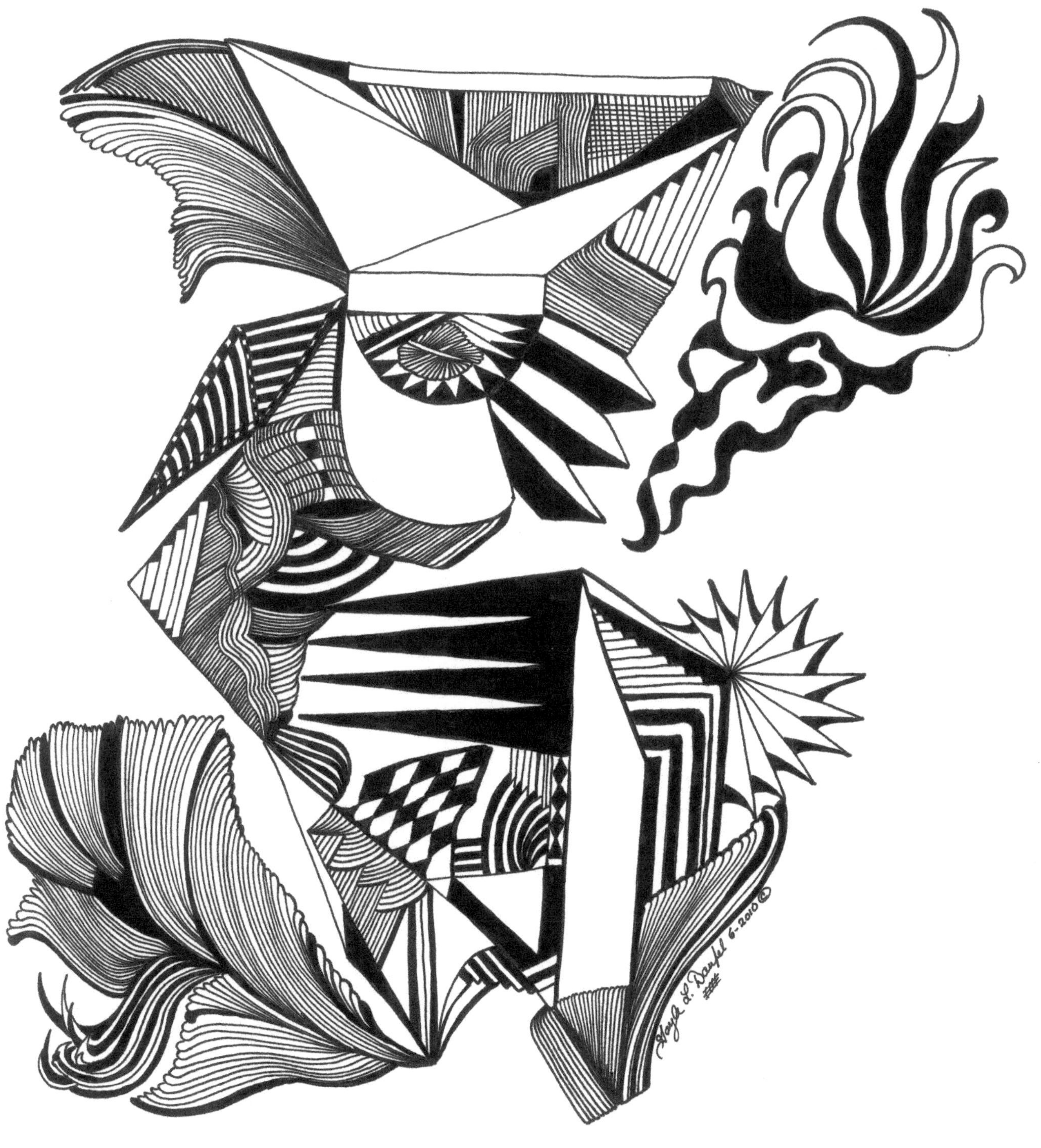

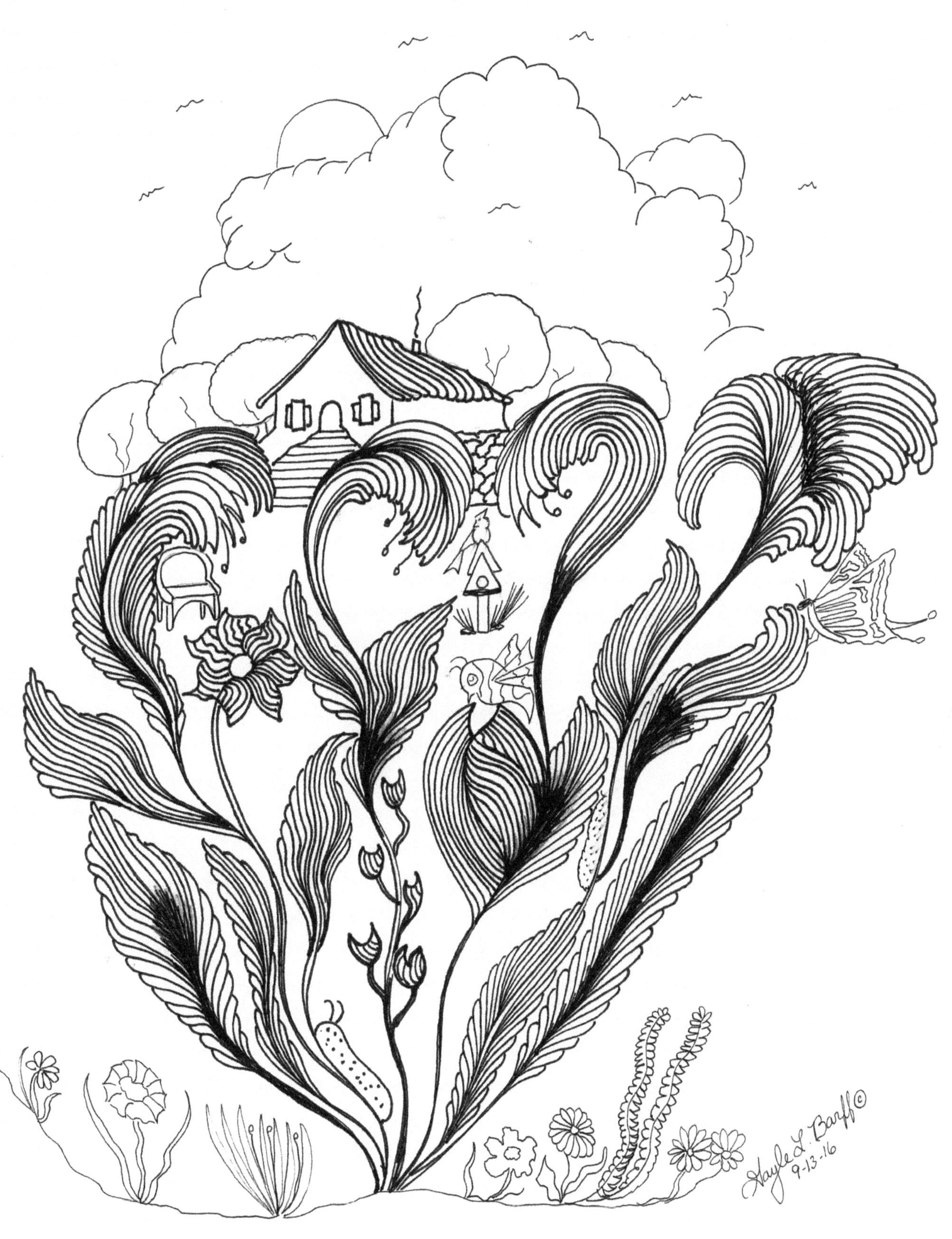

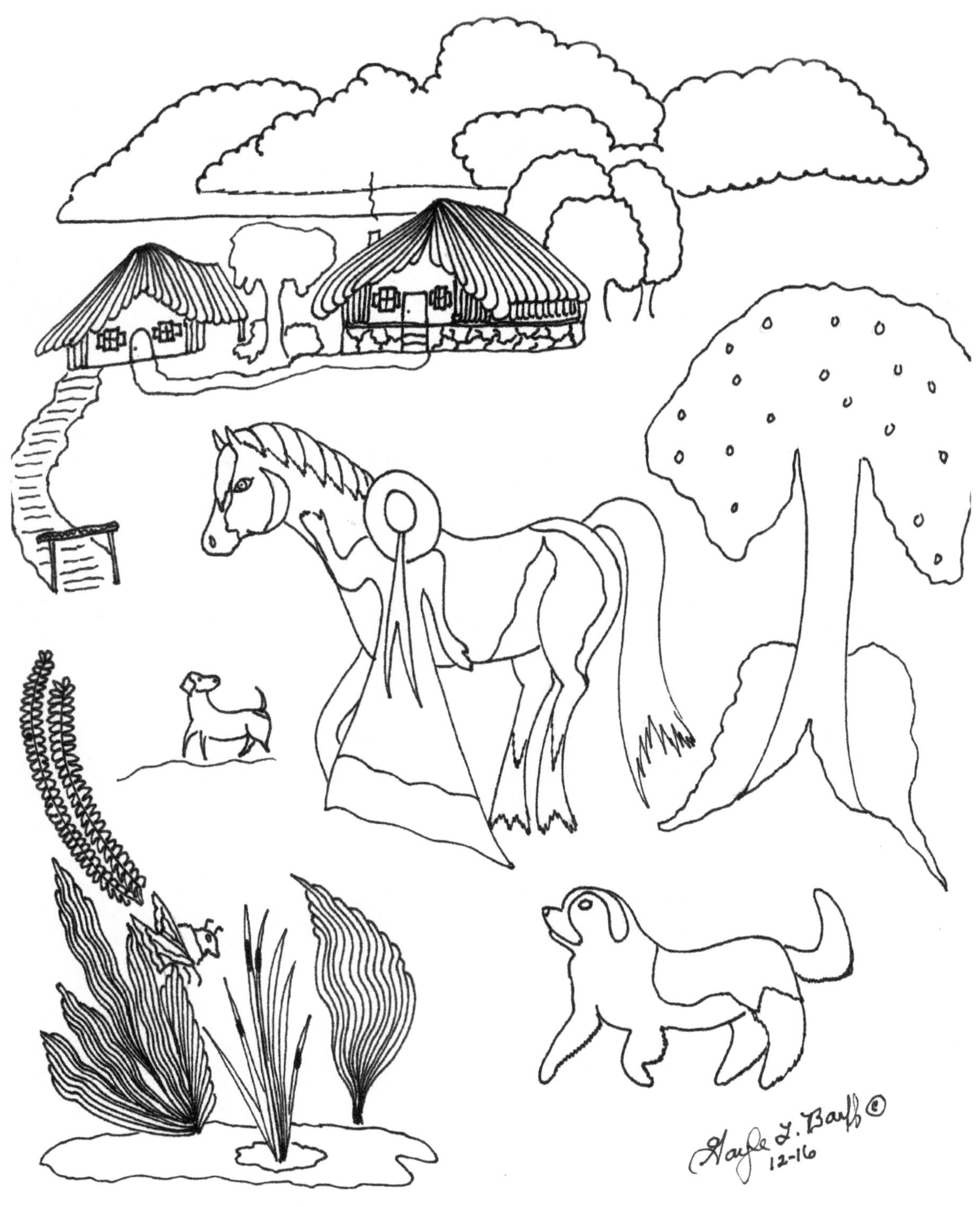

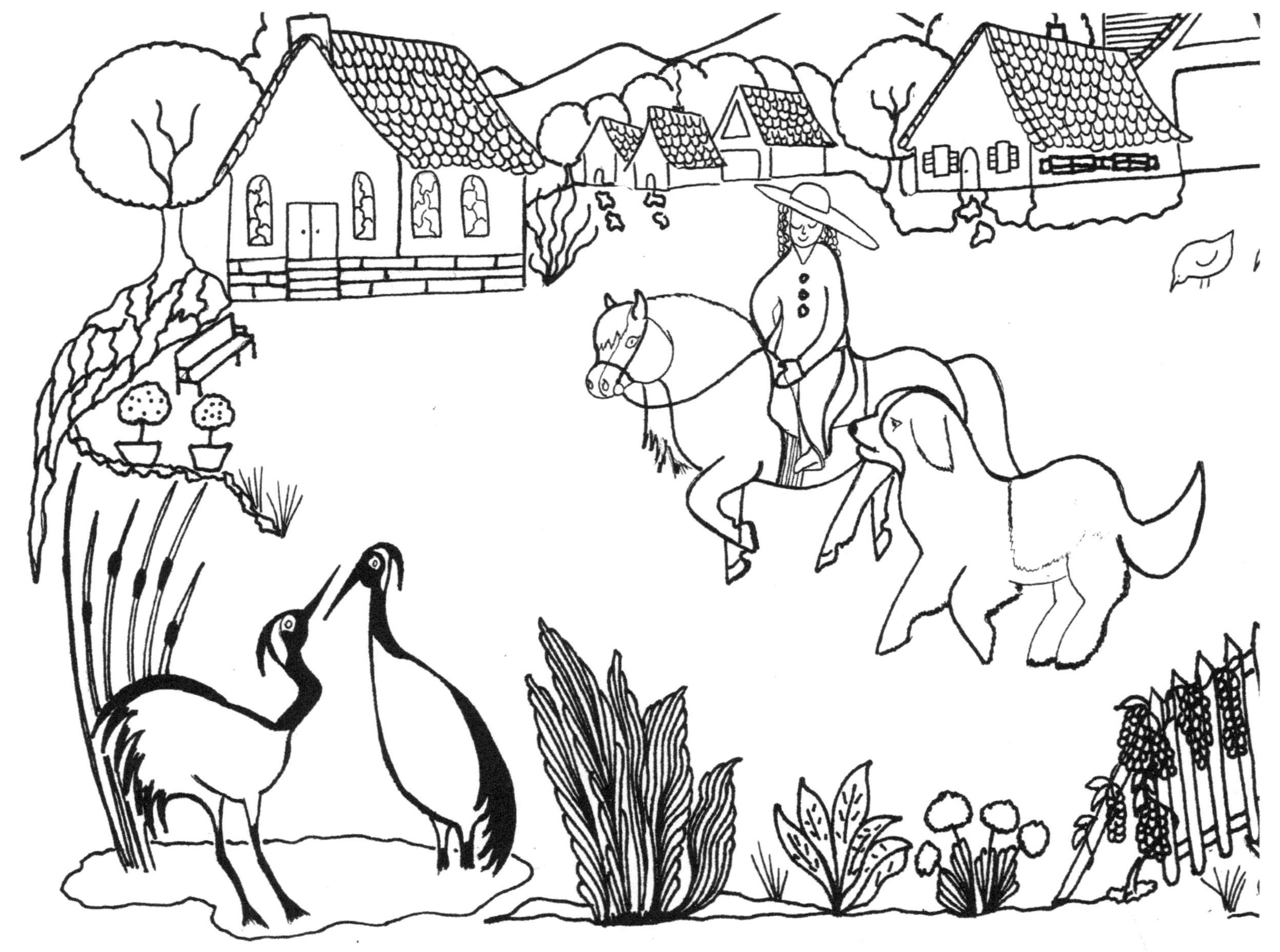

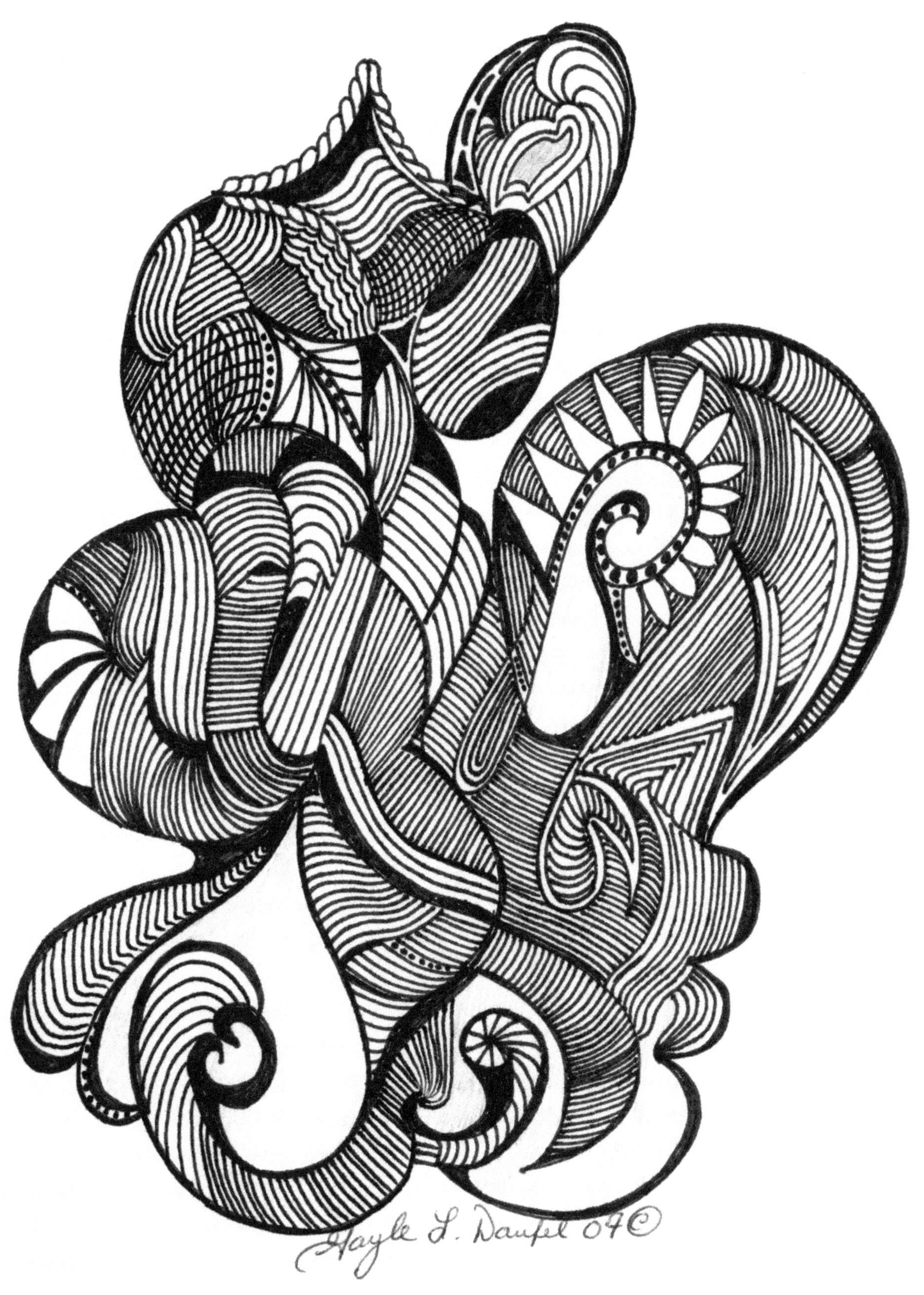

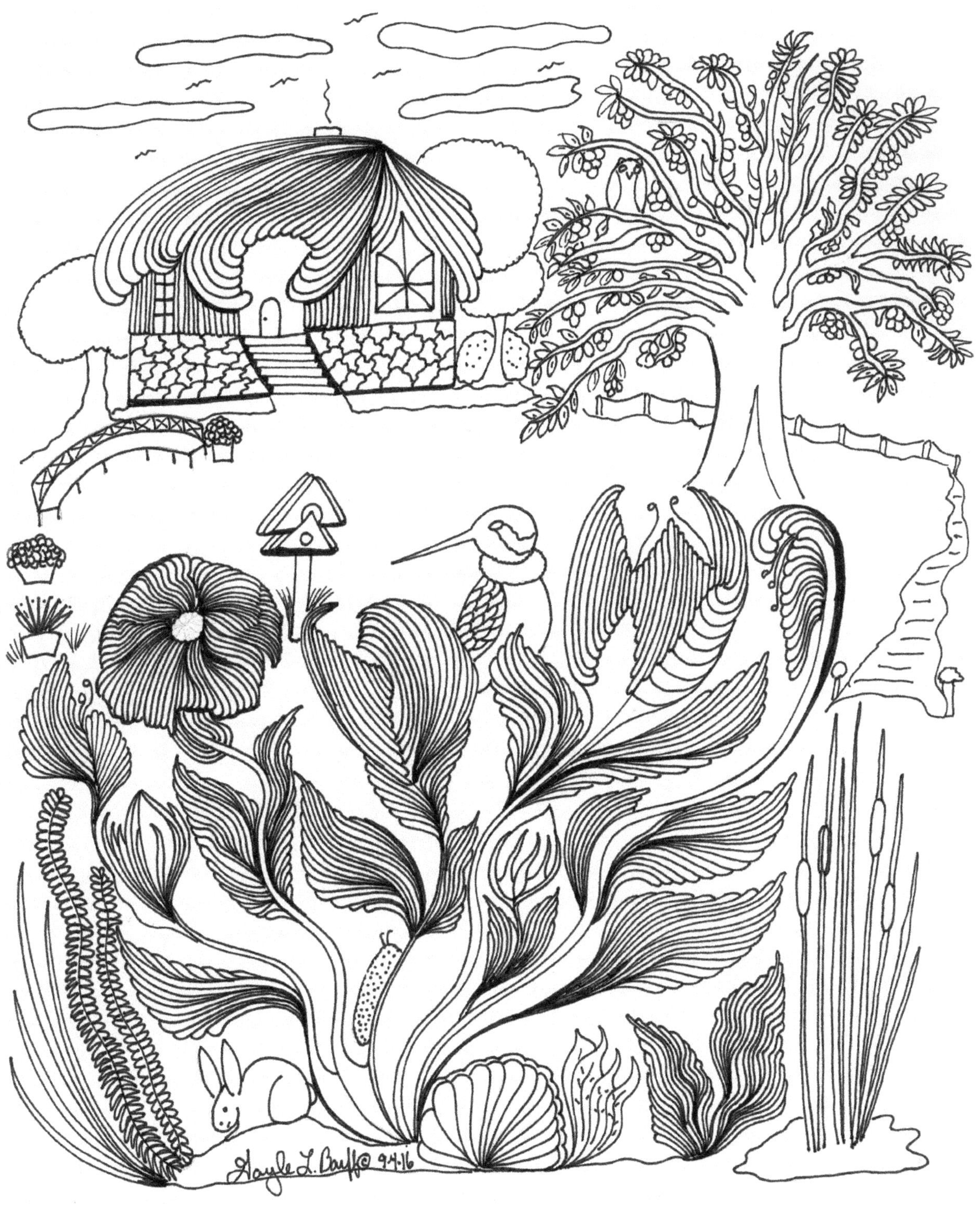

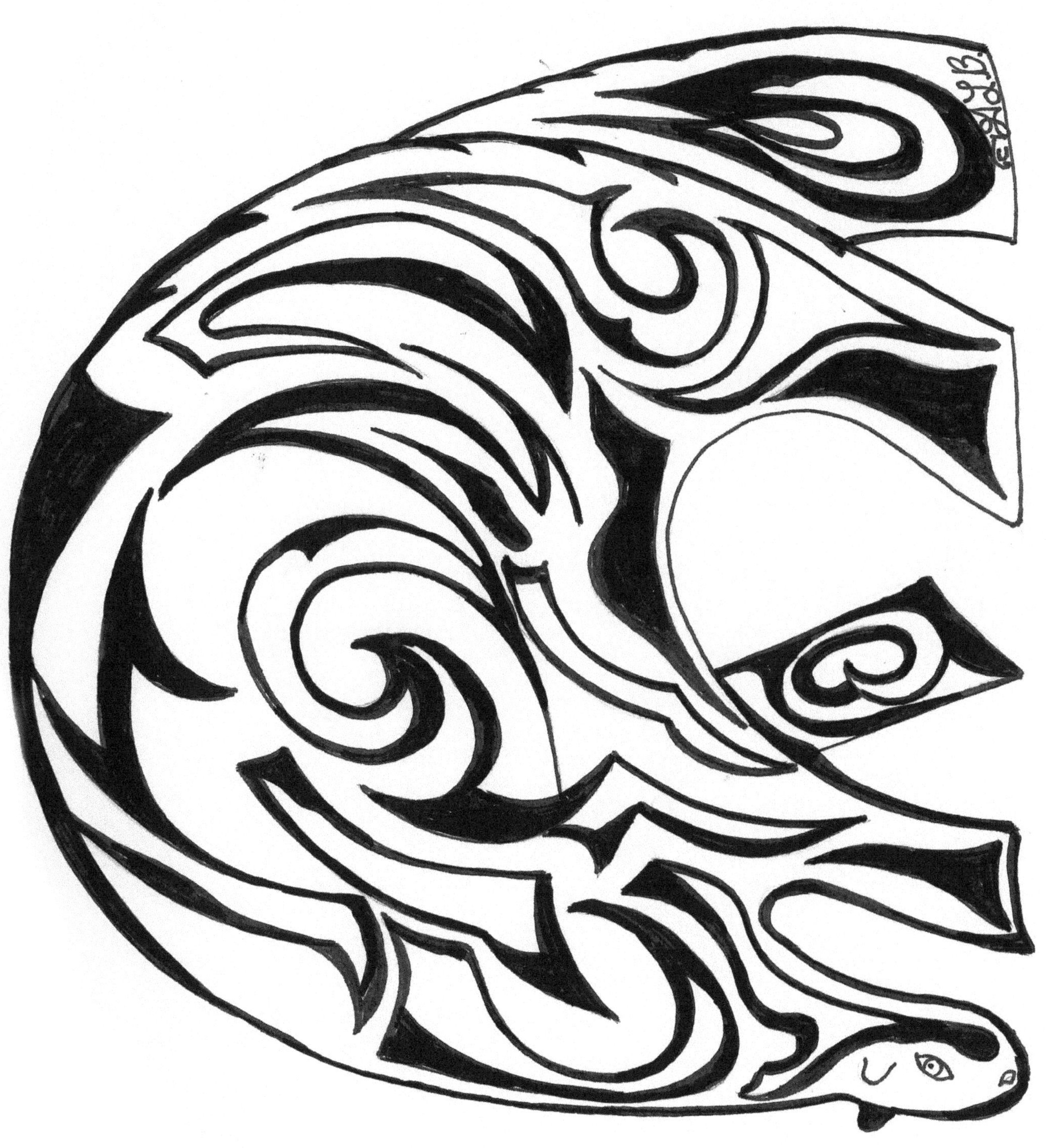

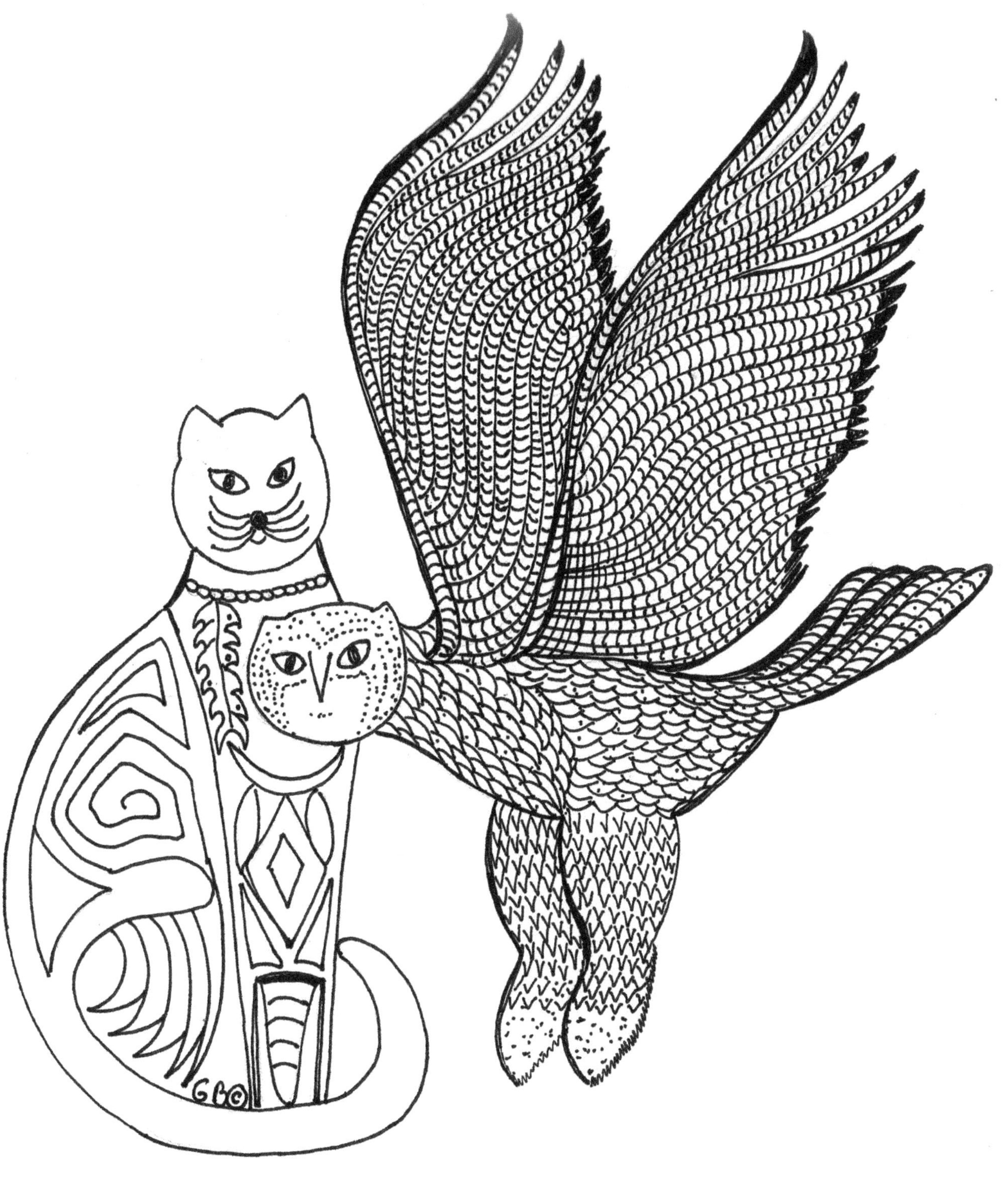

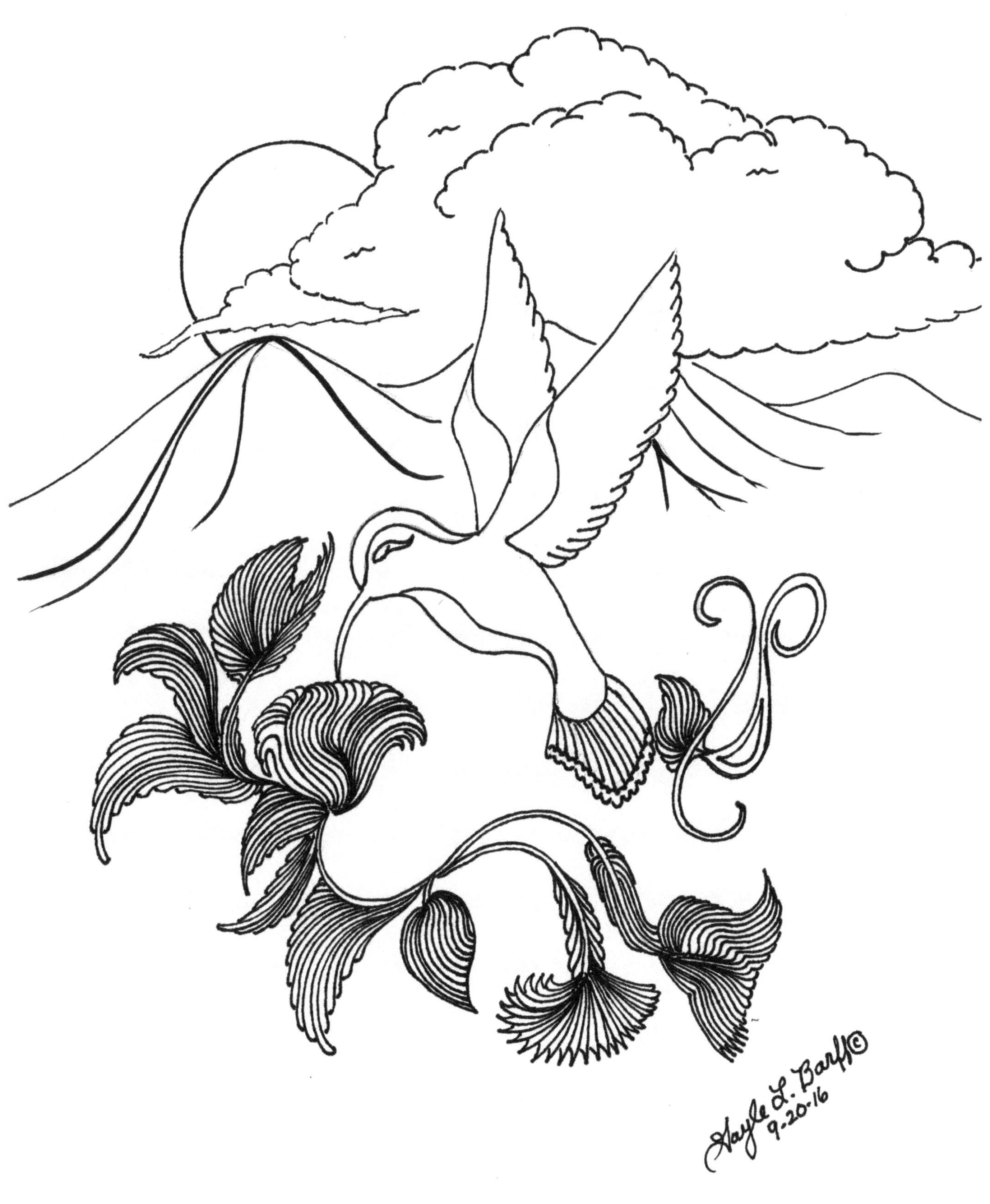

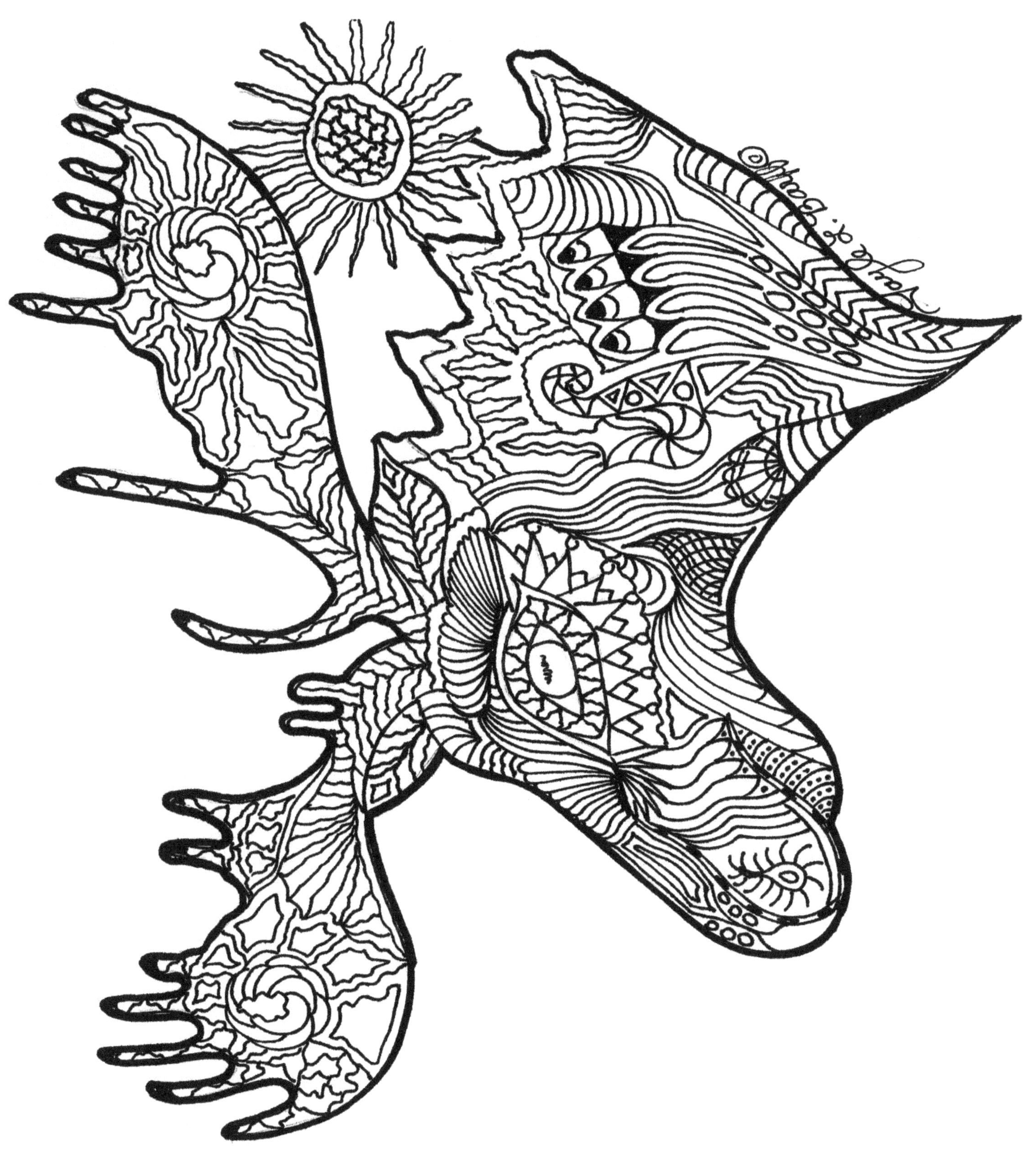

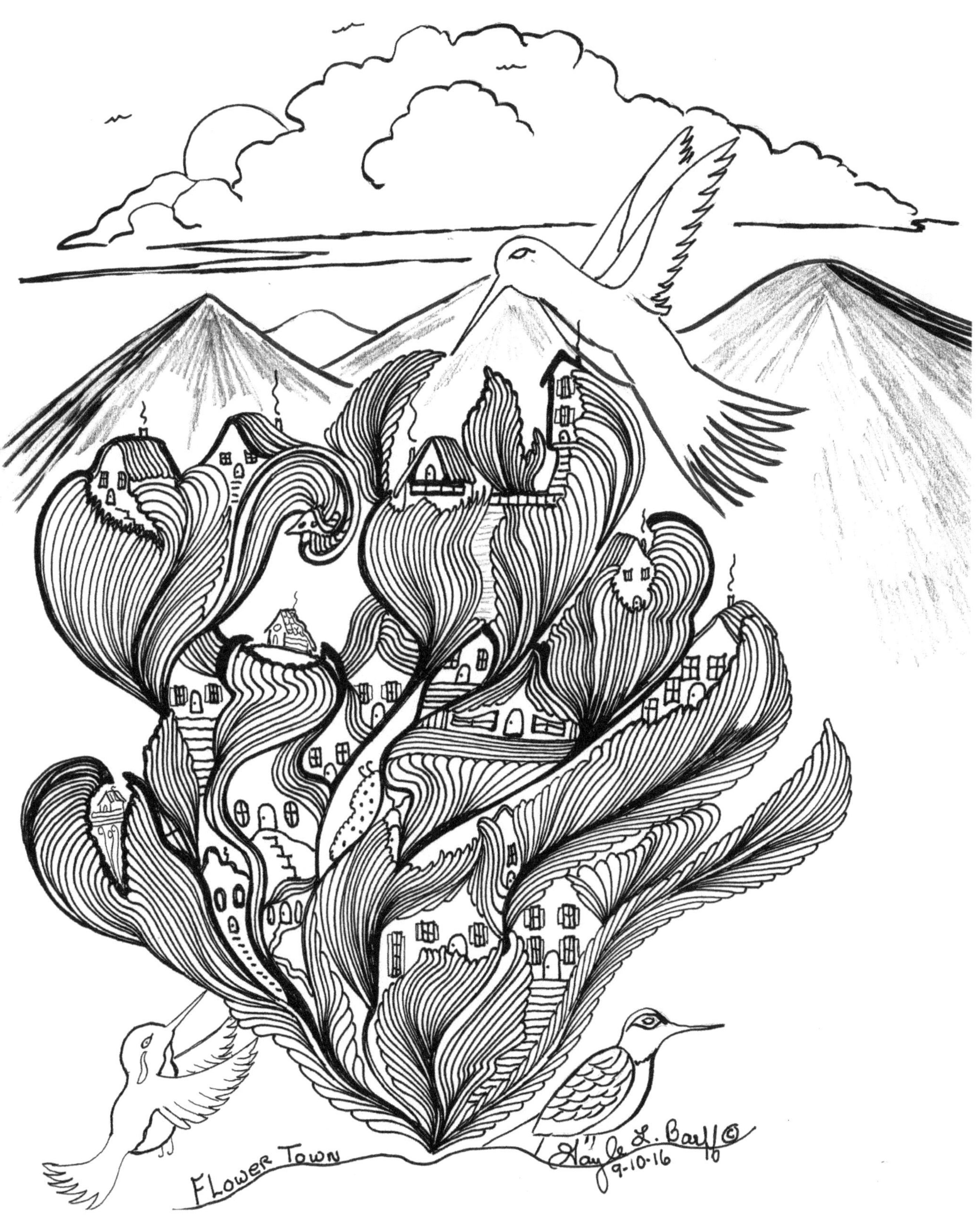

Flower Town
Gayle L. Barff ©
9-10-16

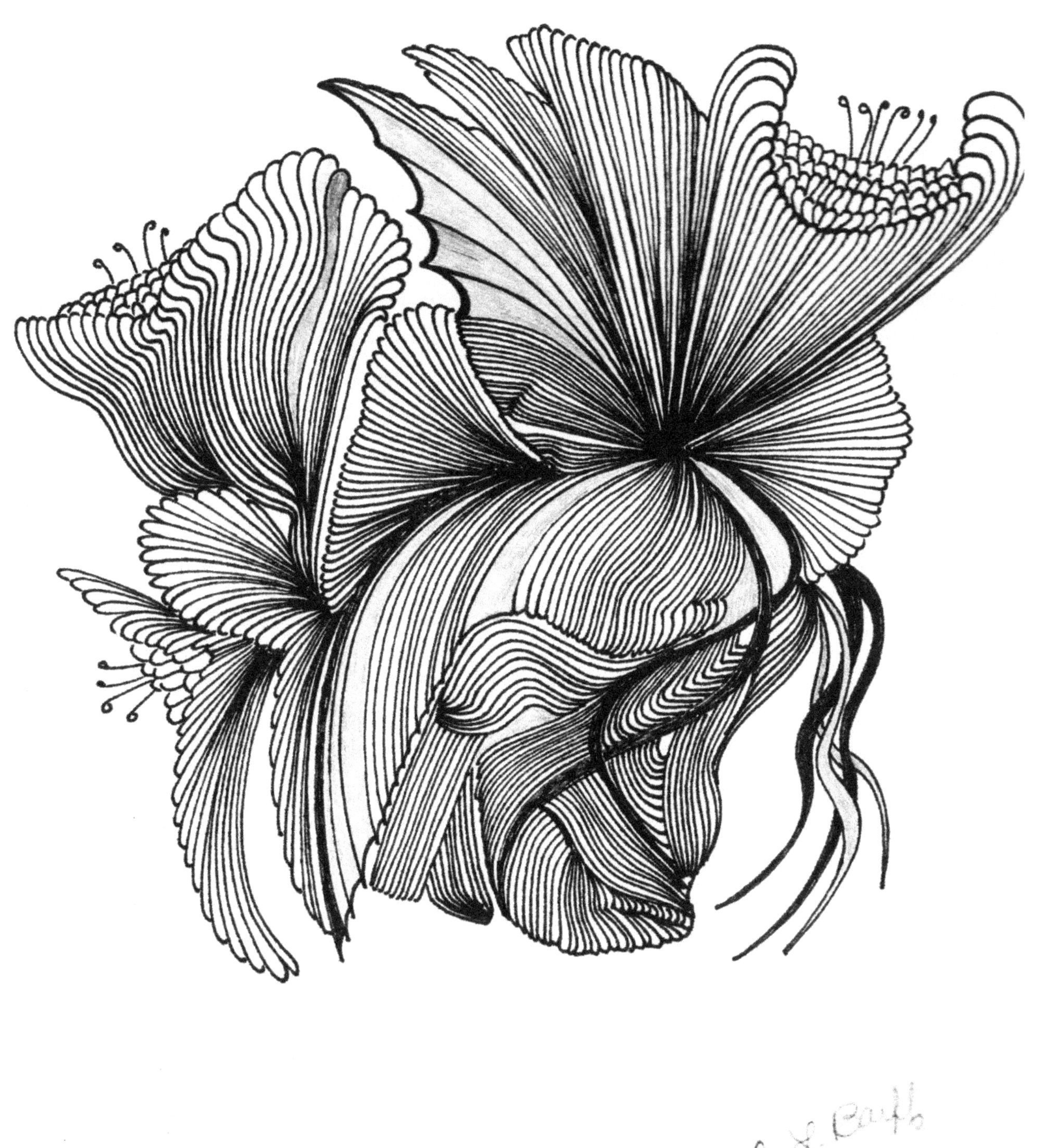

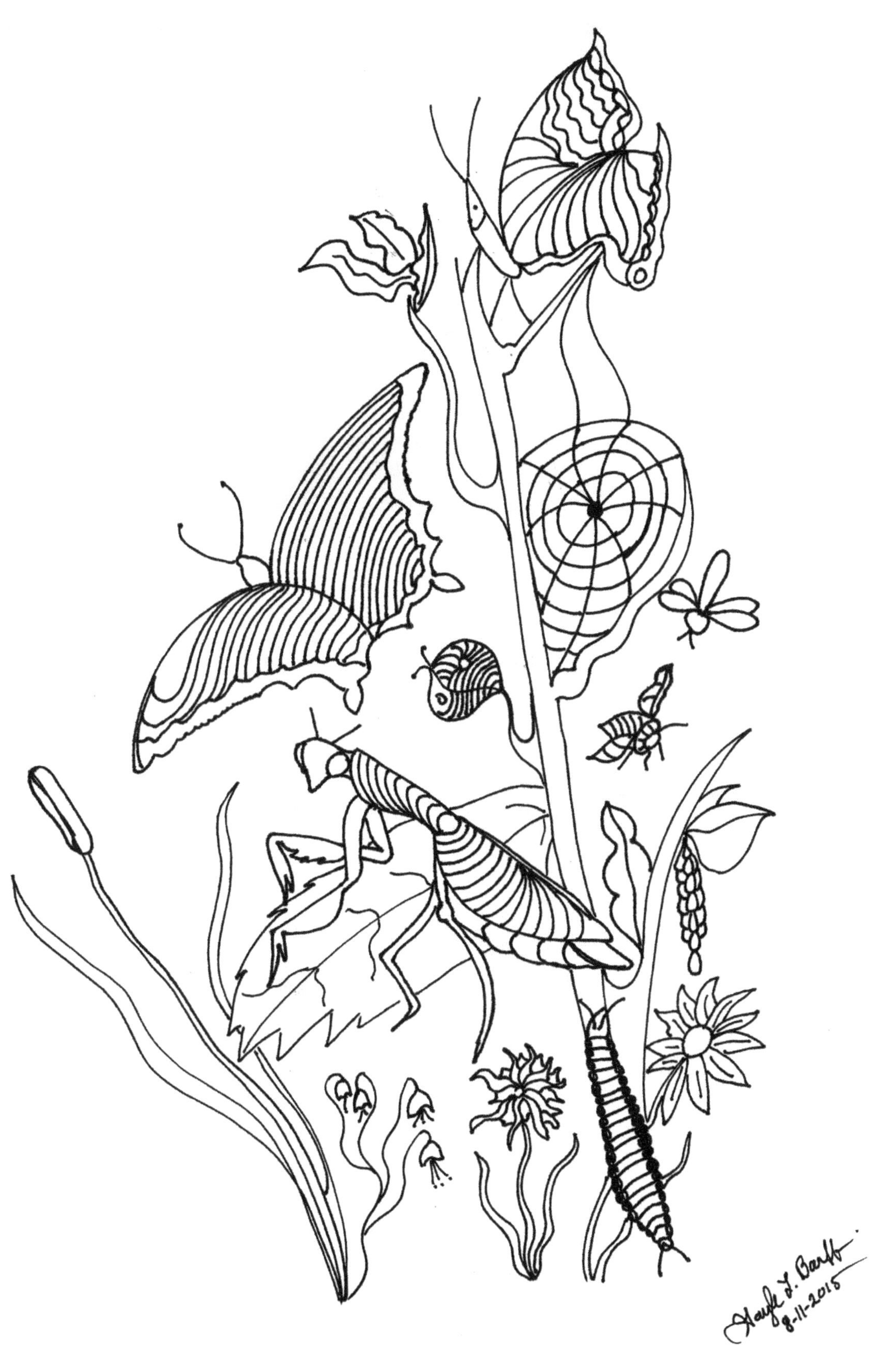

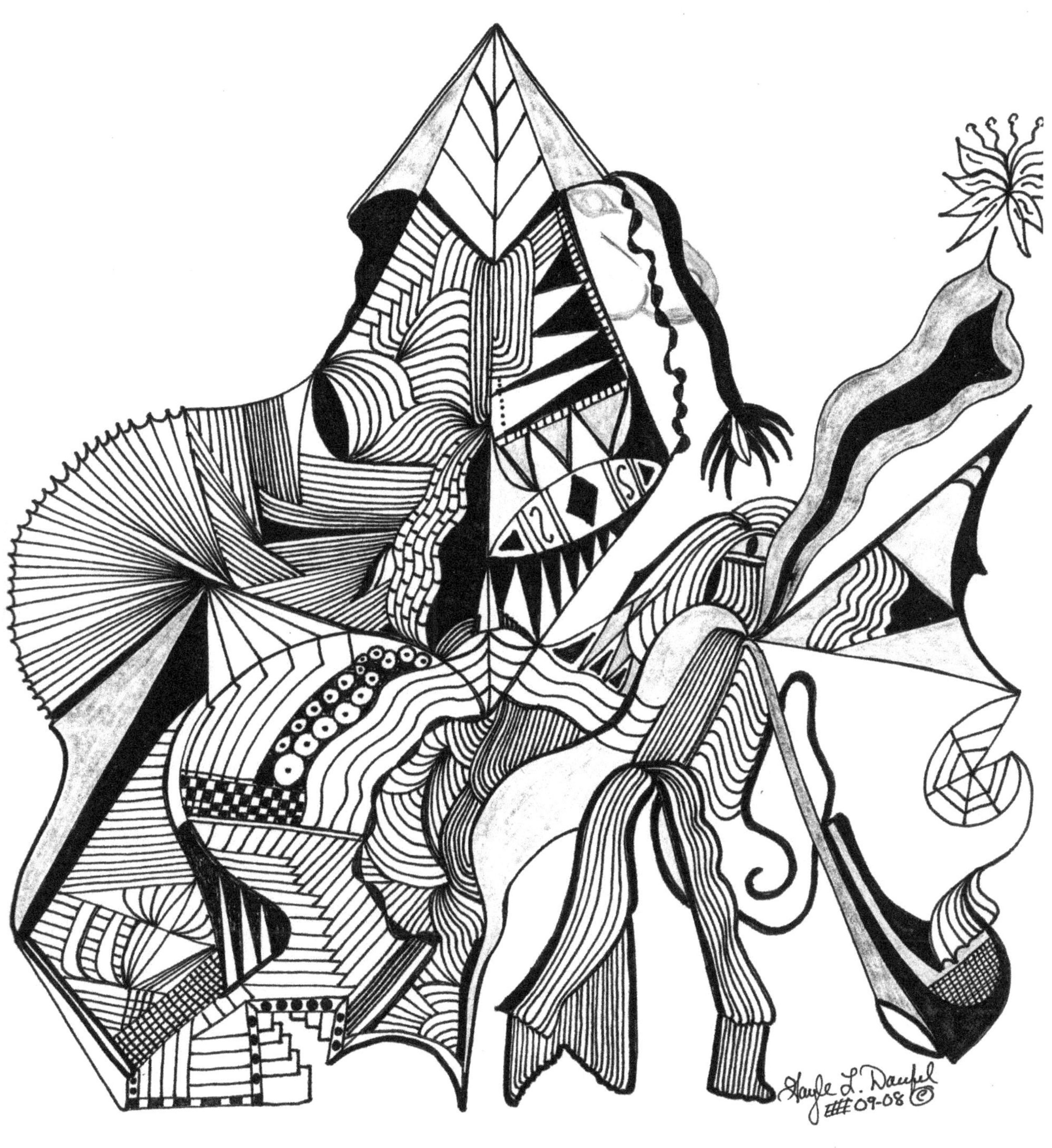

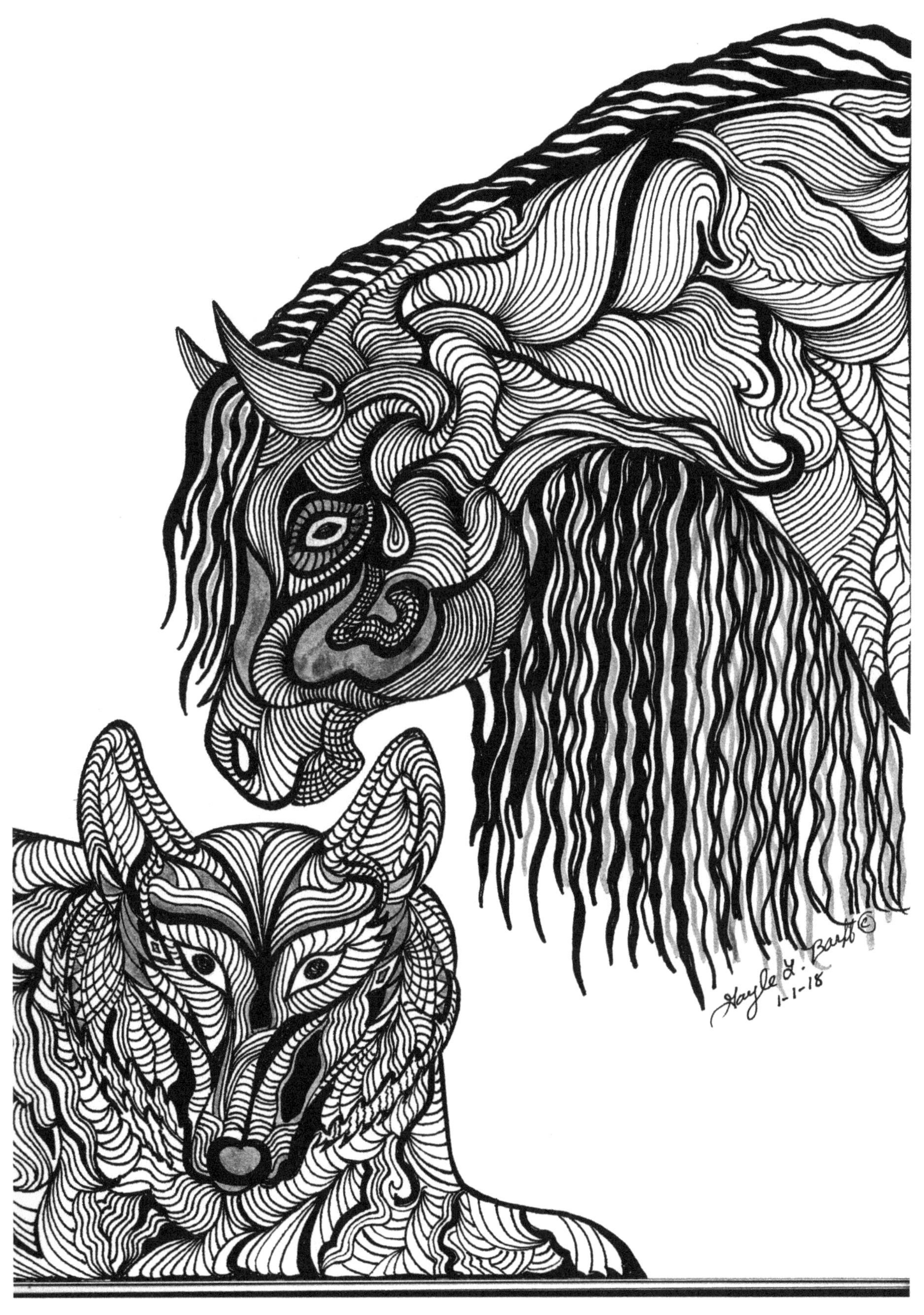

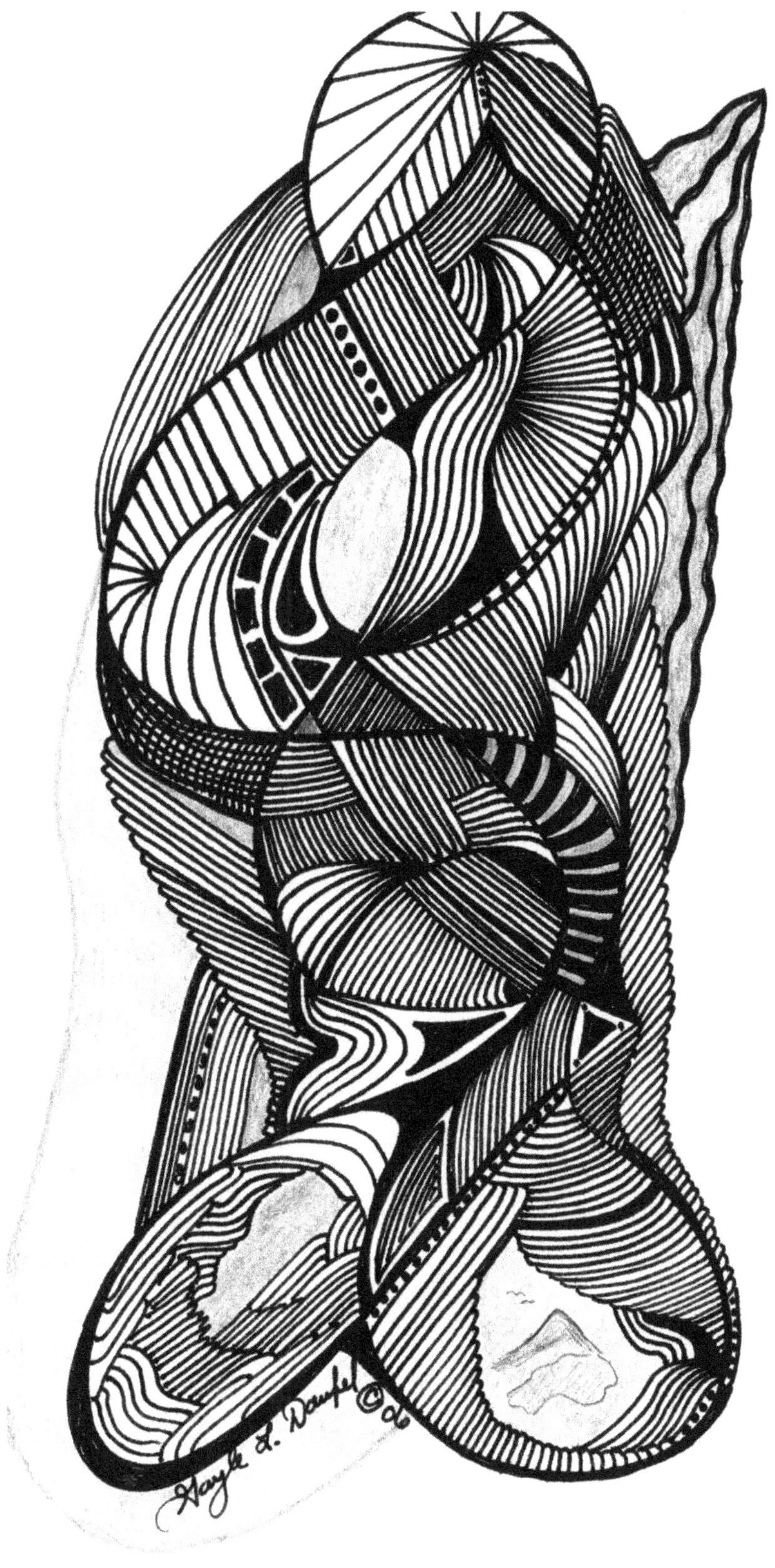

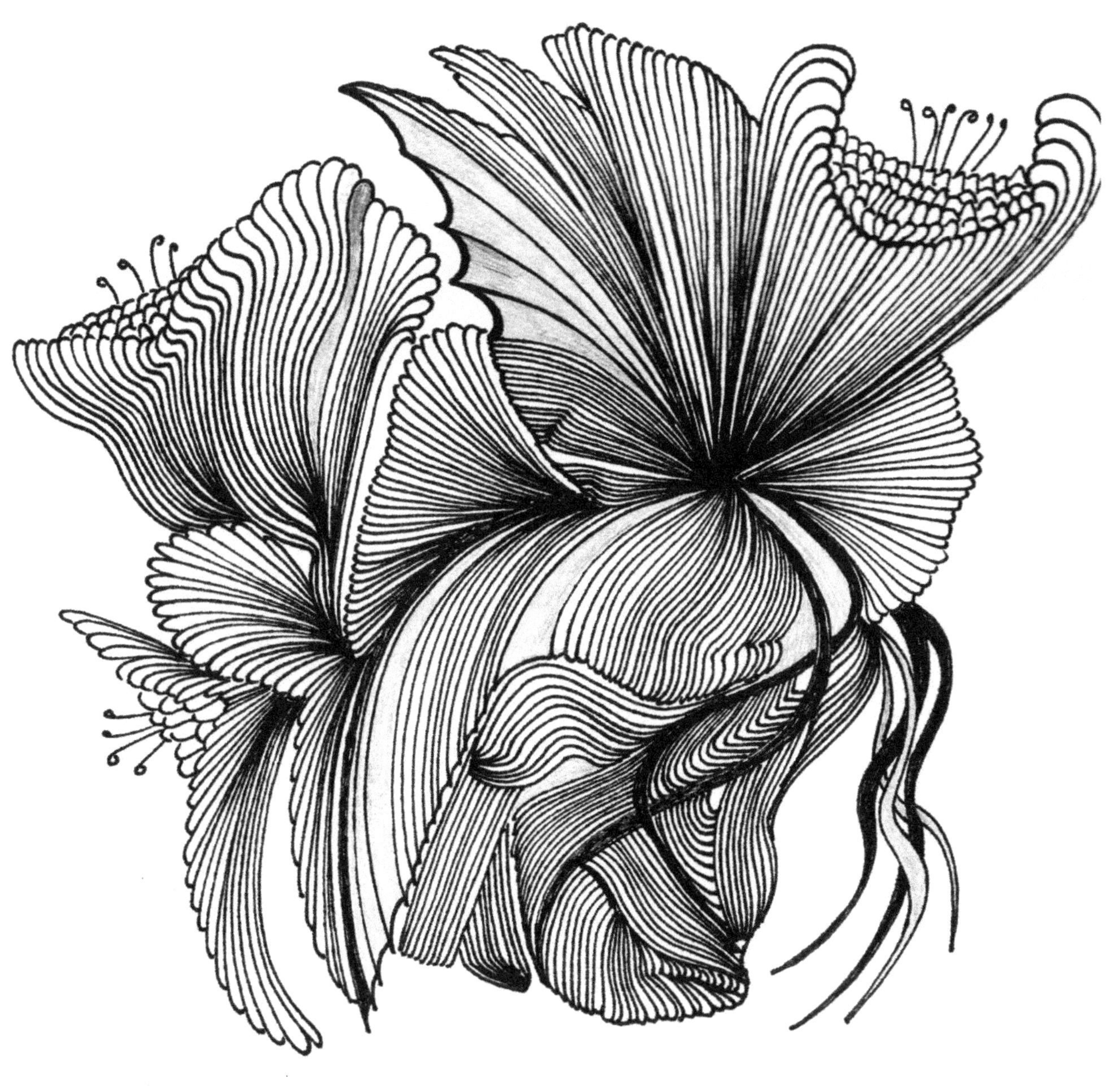

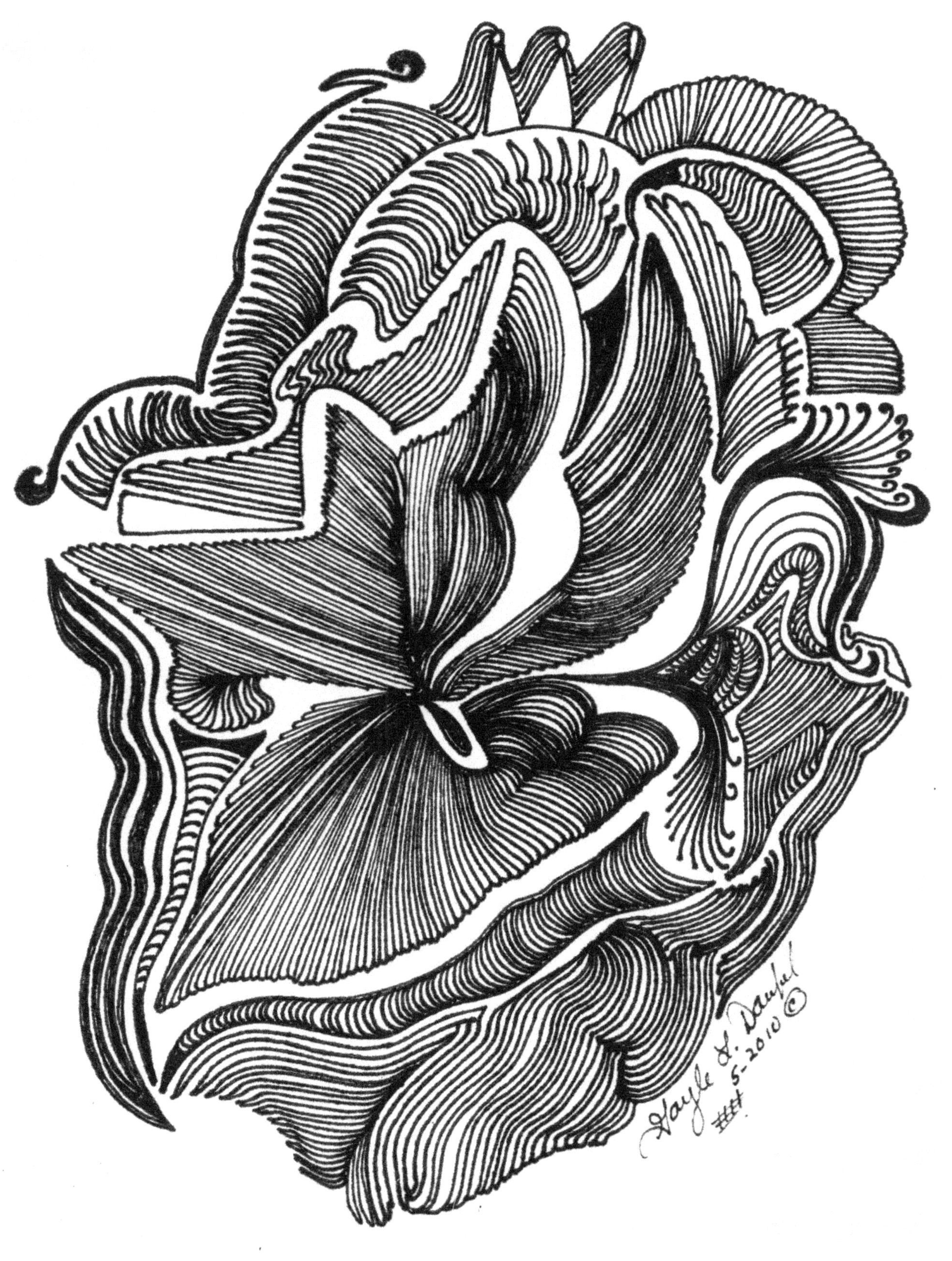

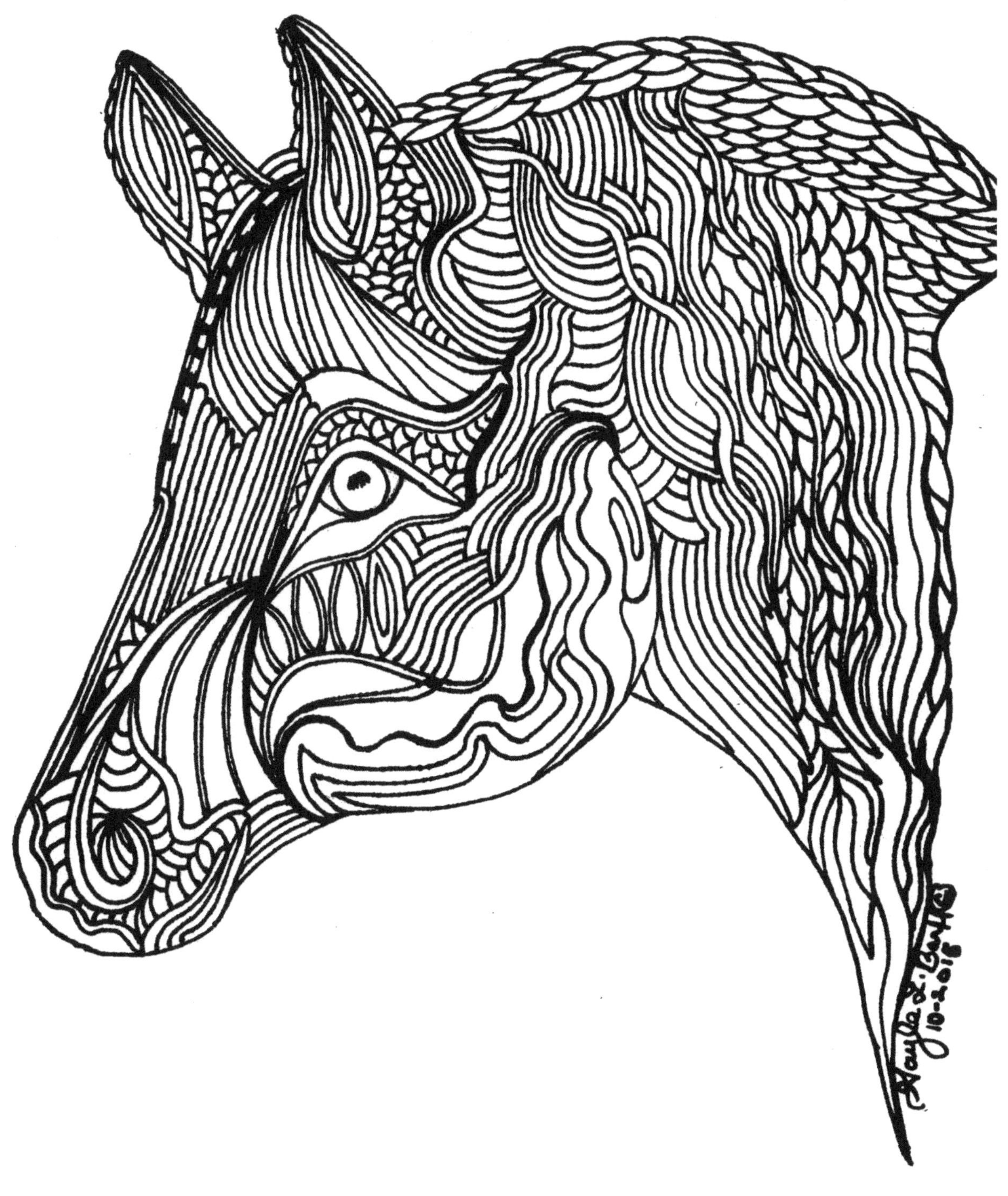

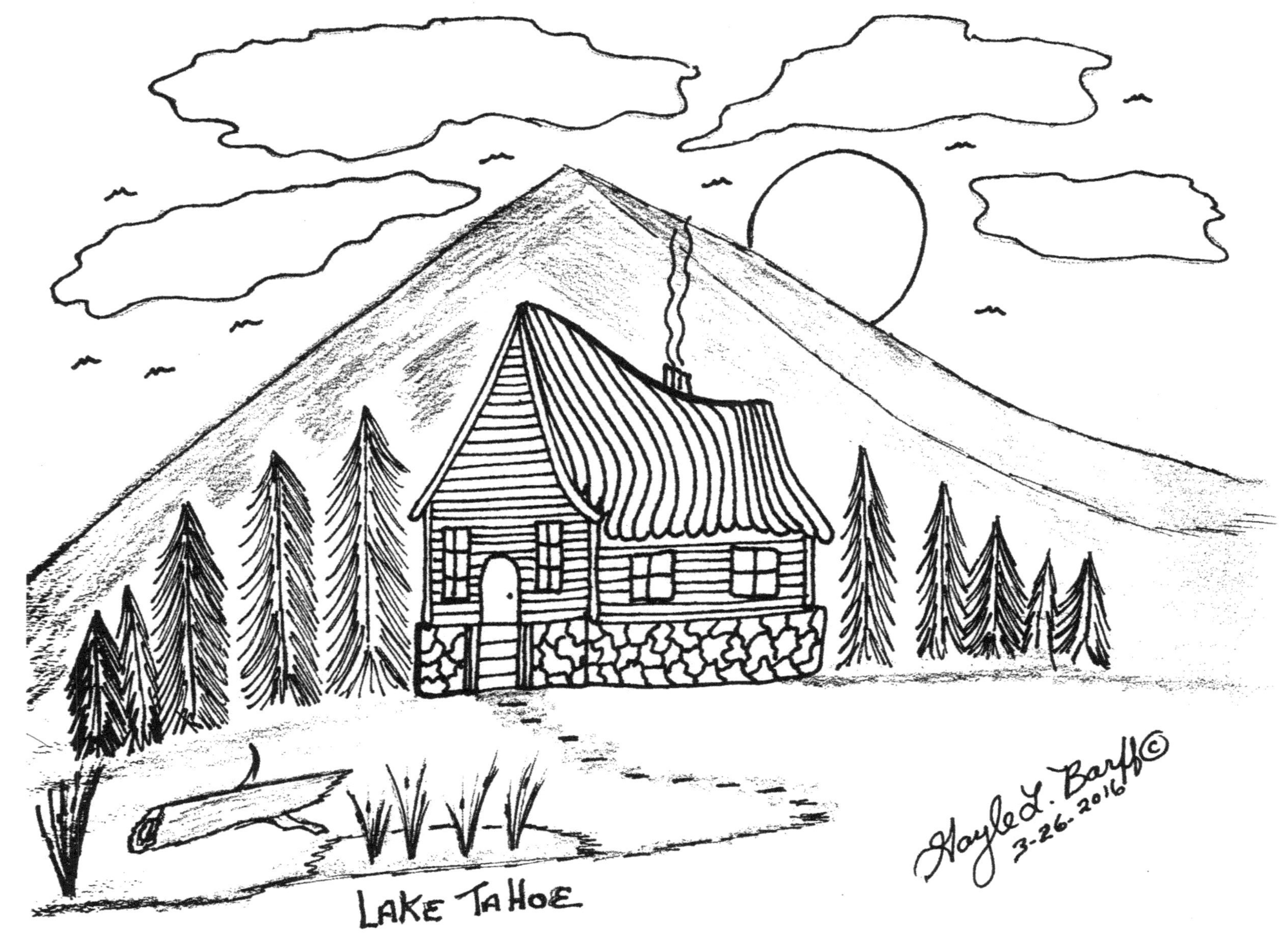
Lake Tahoe

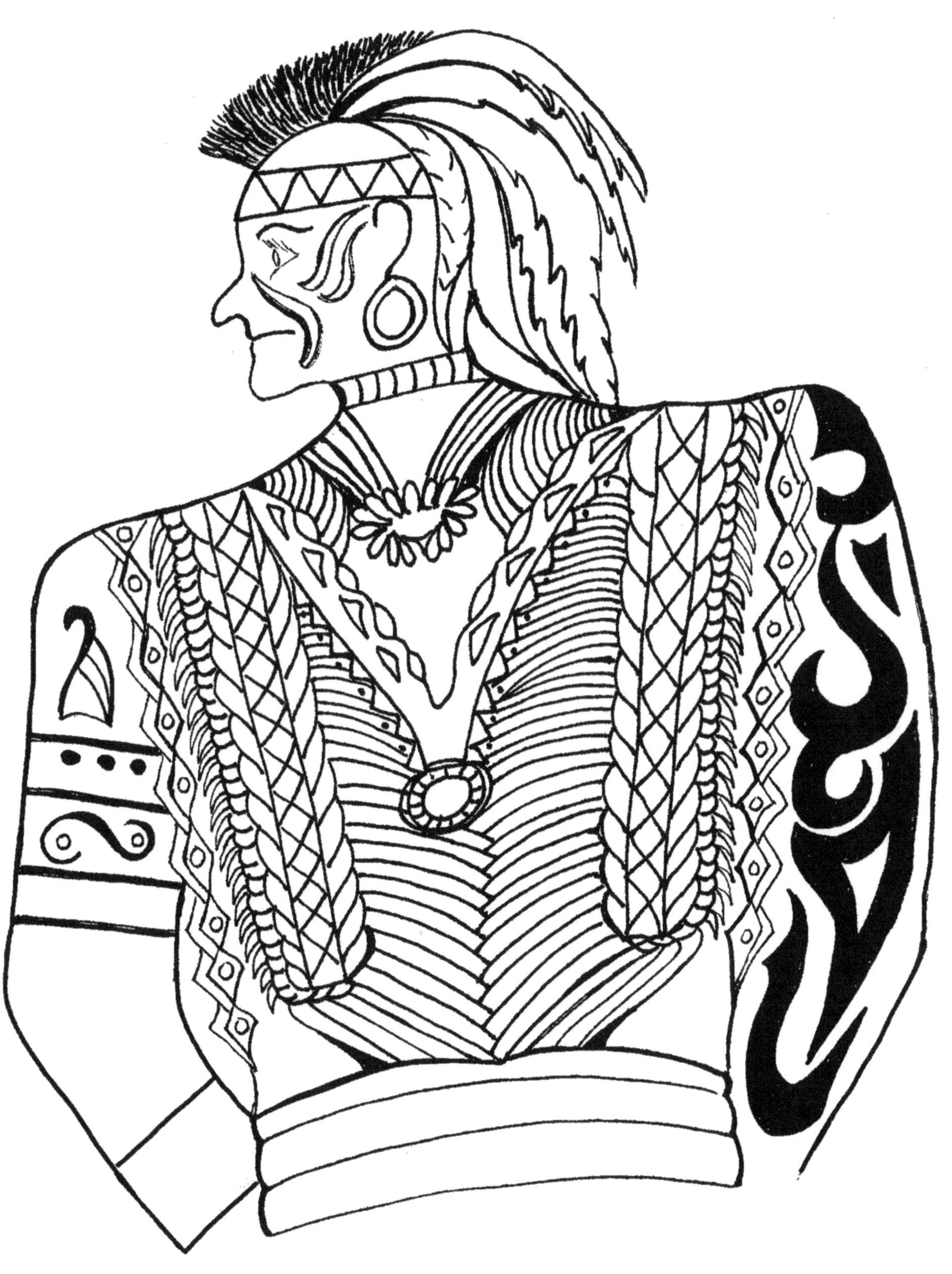

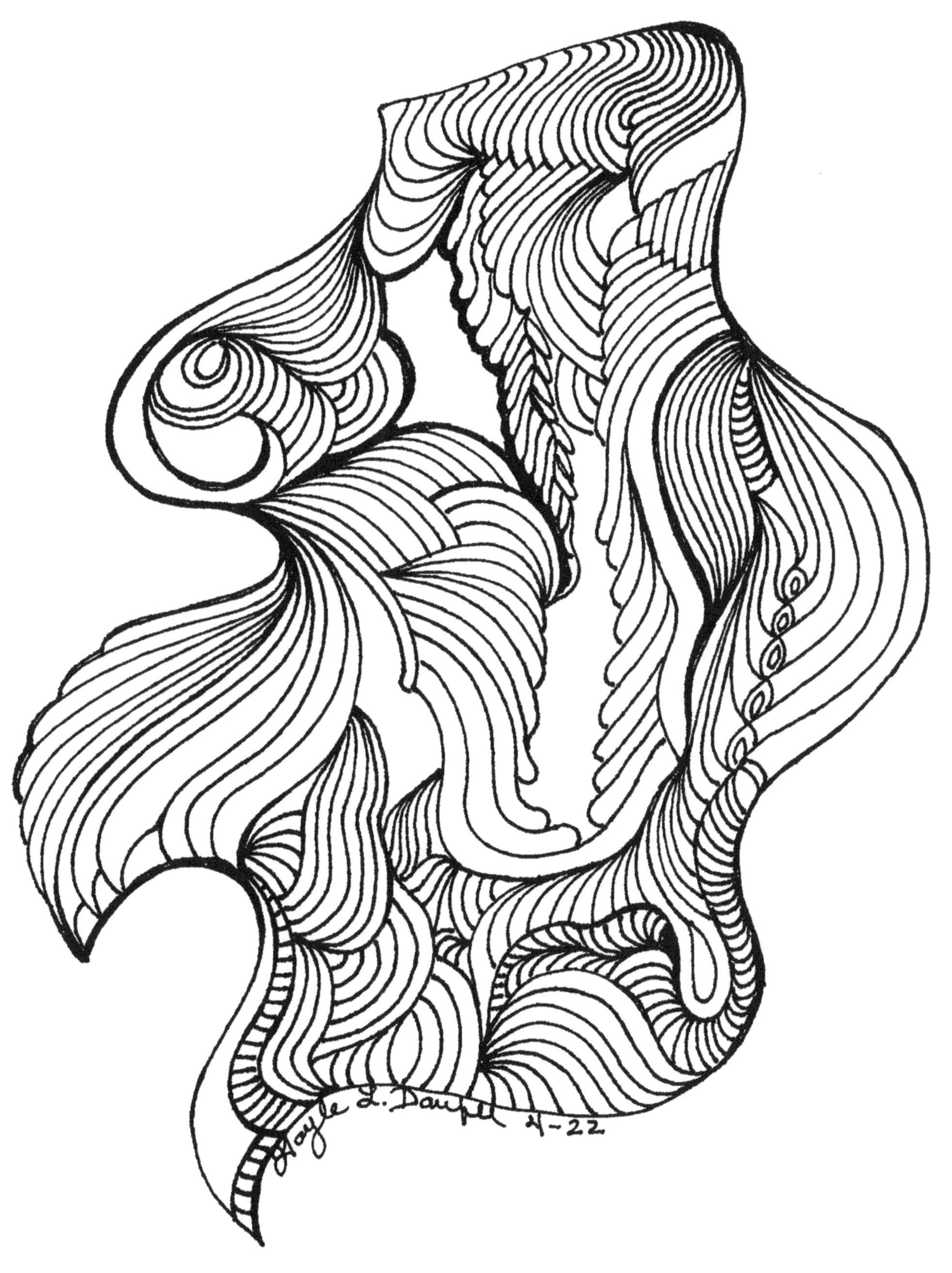

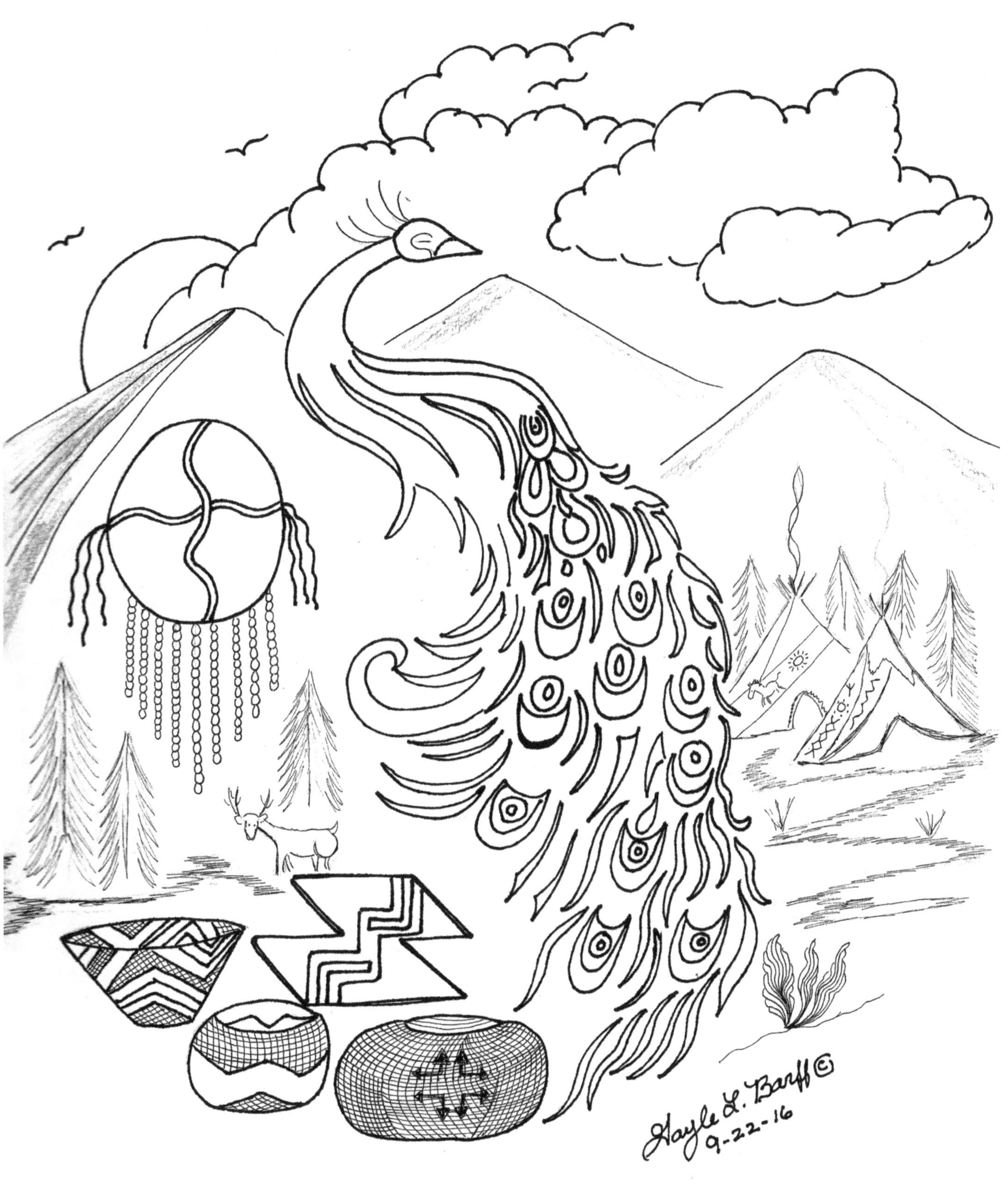

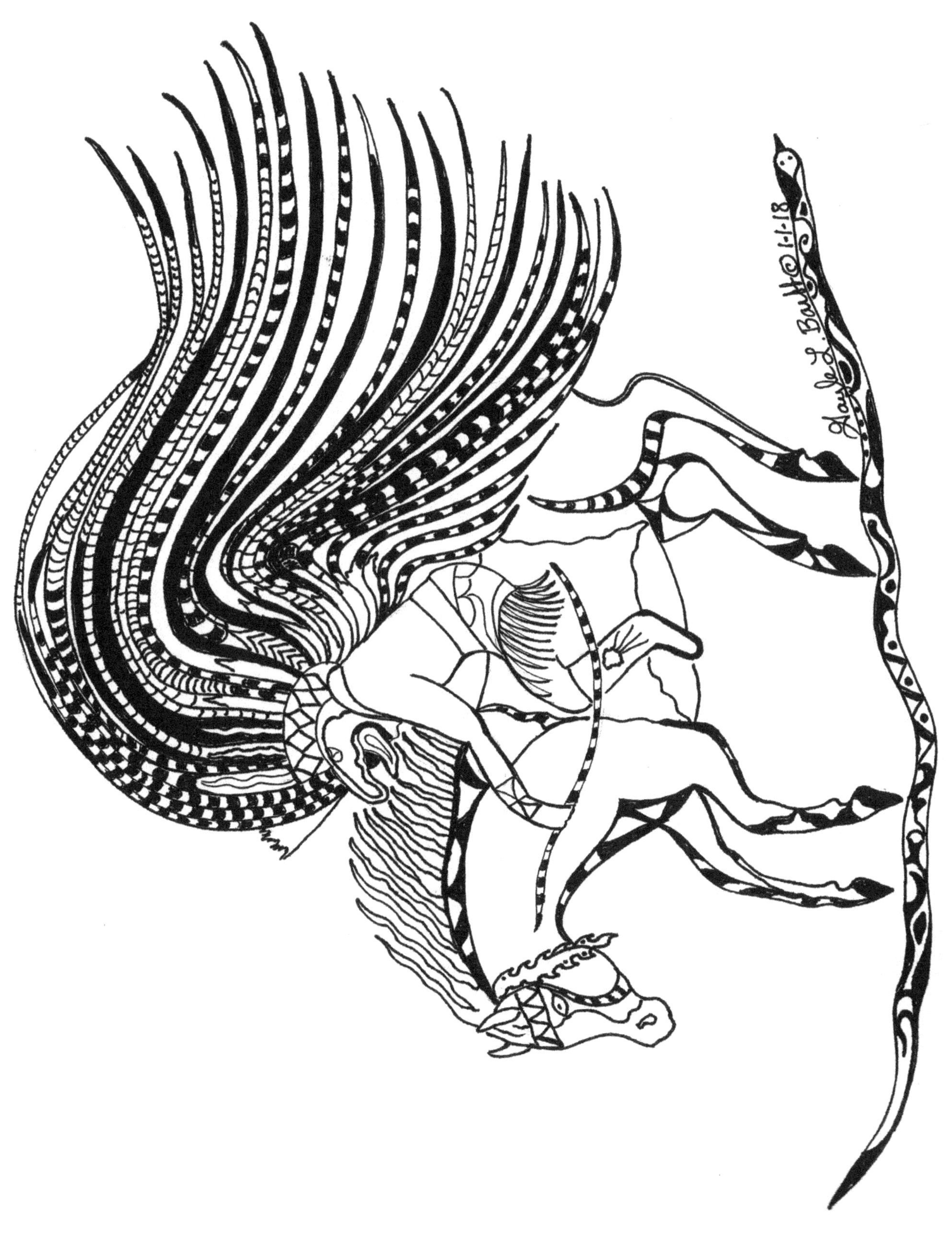

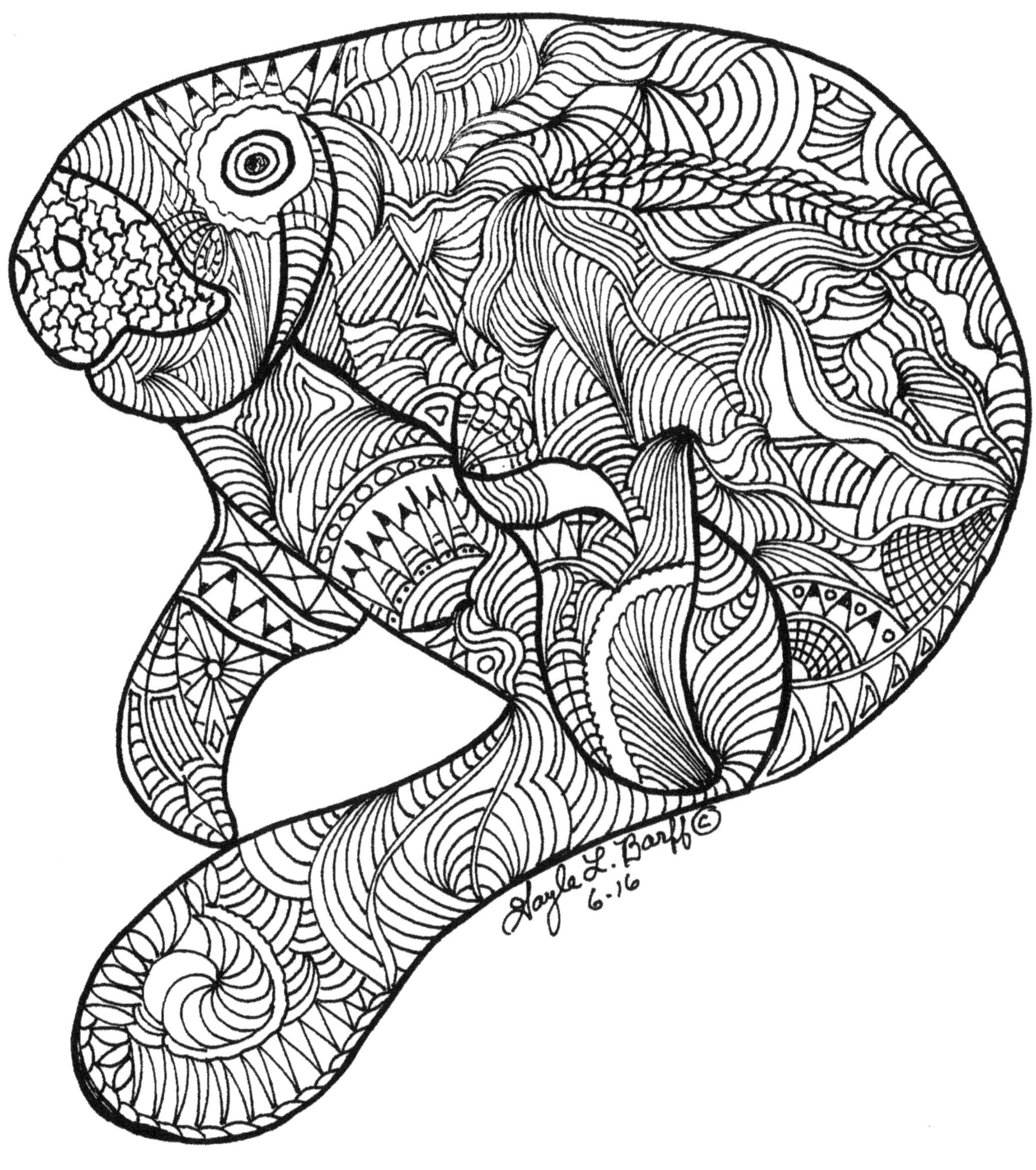

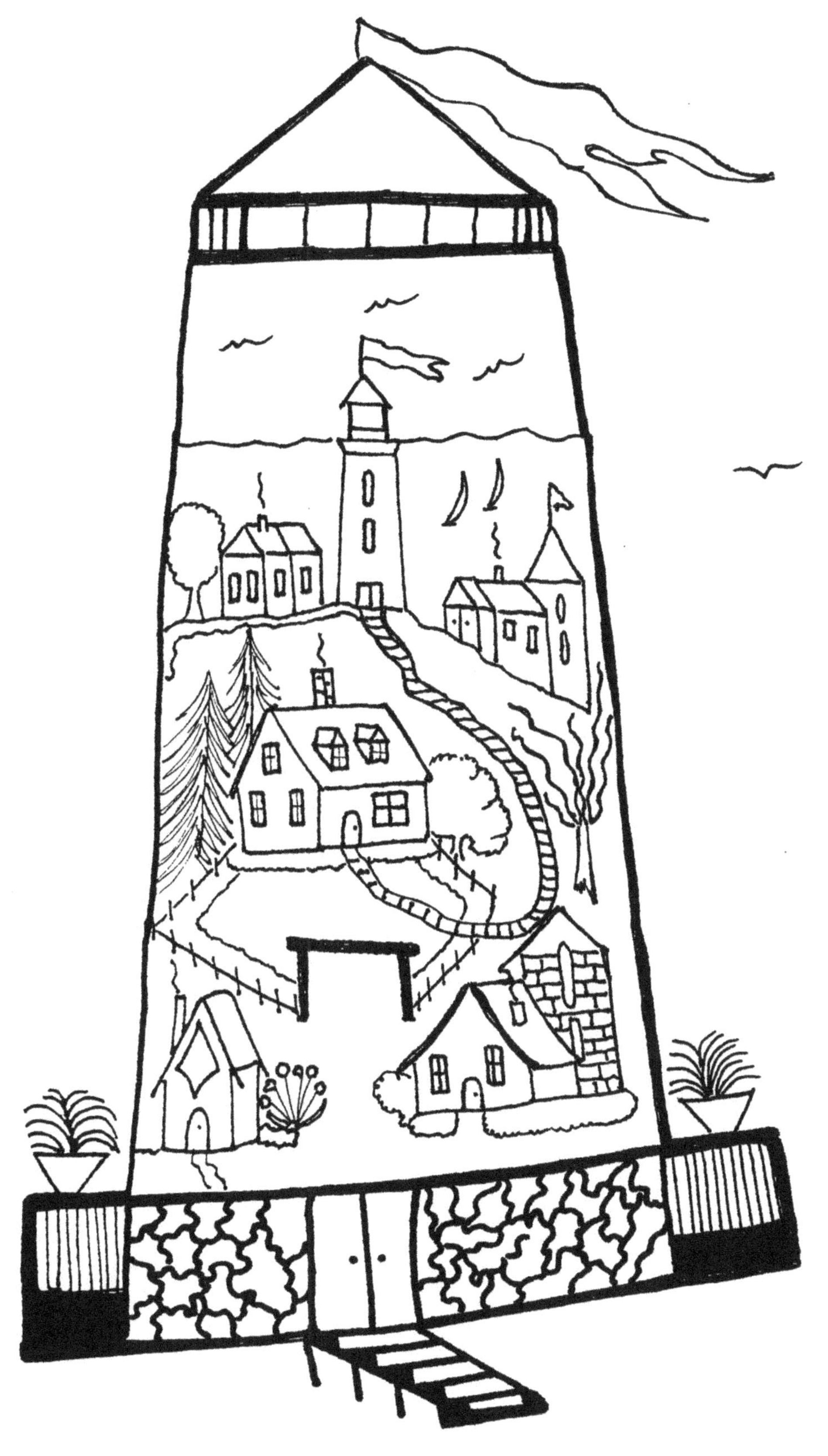

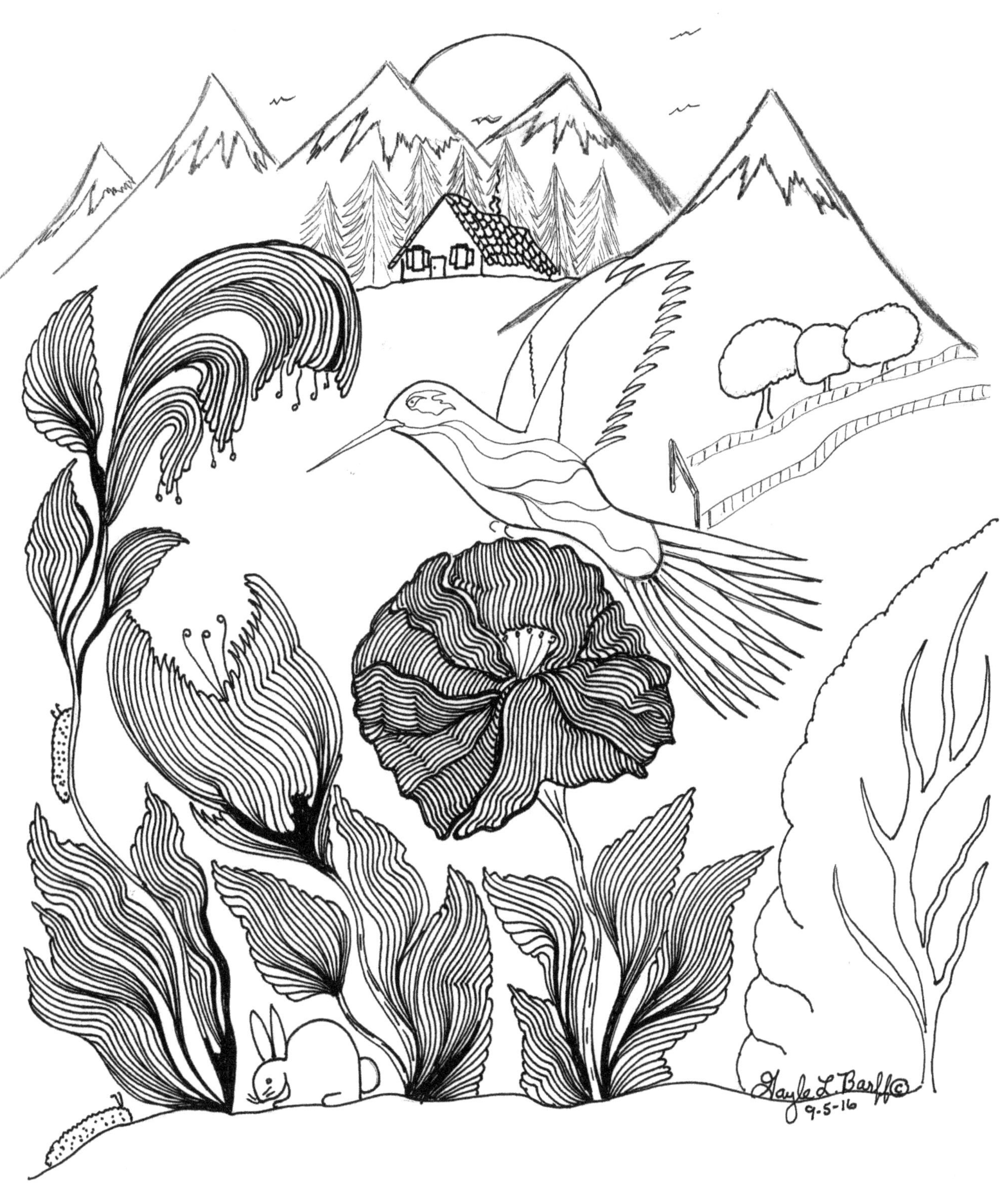

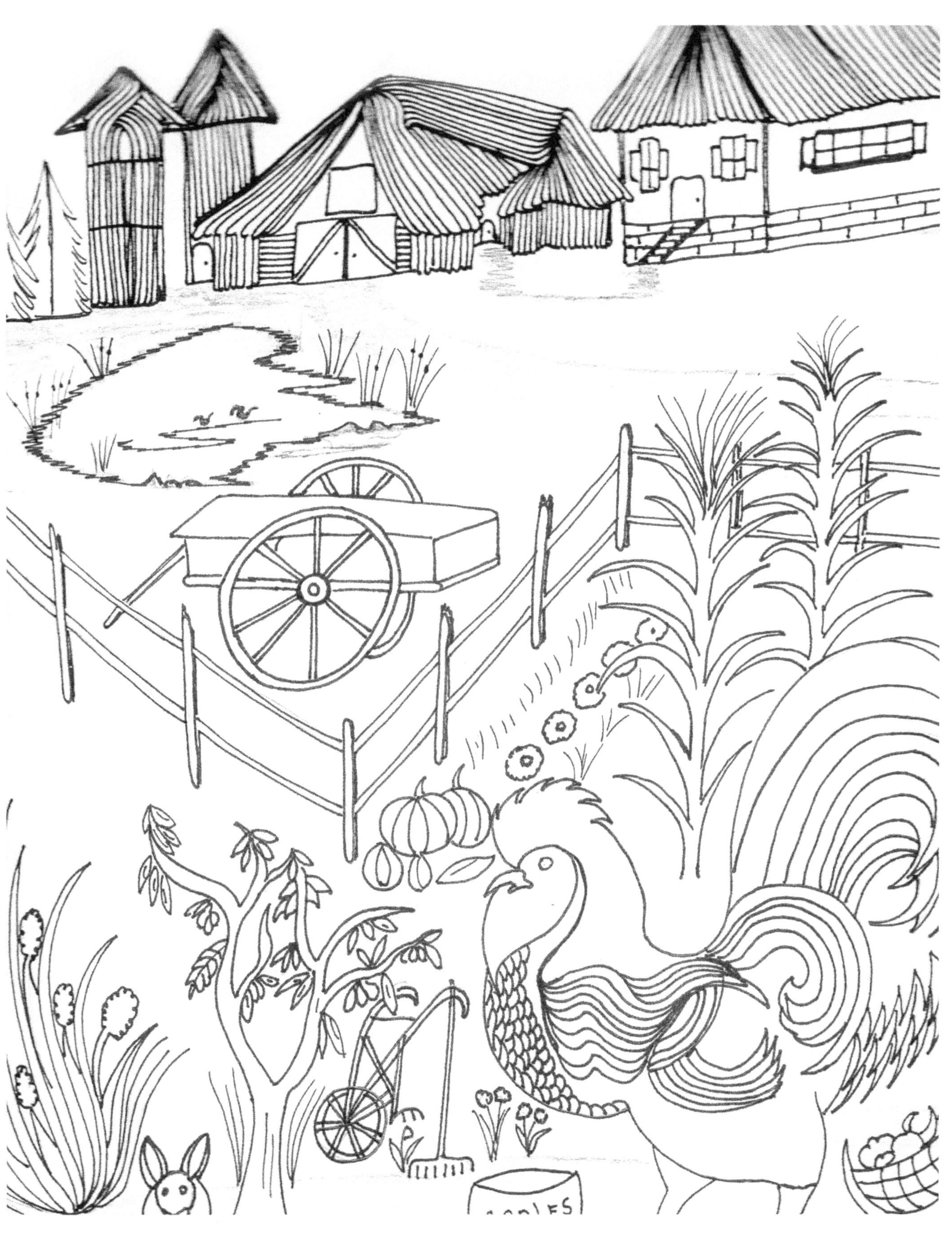

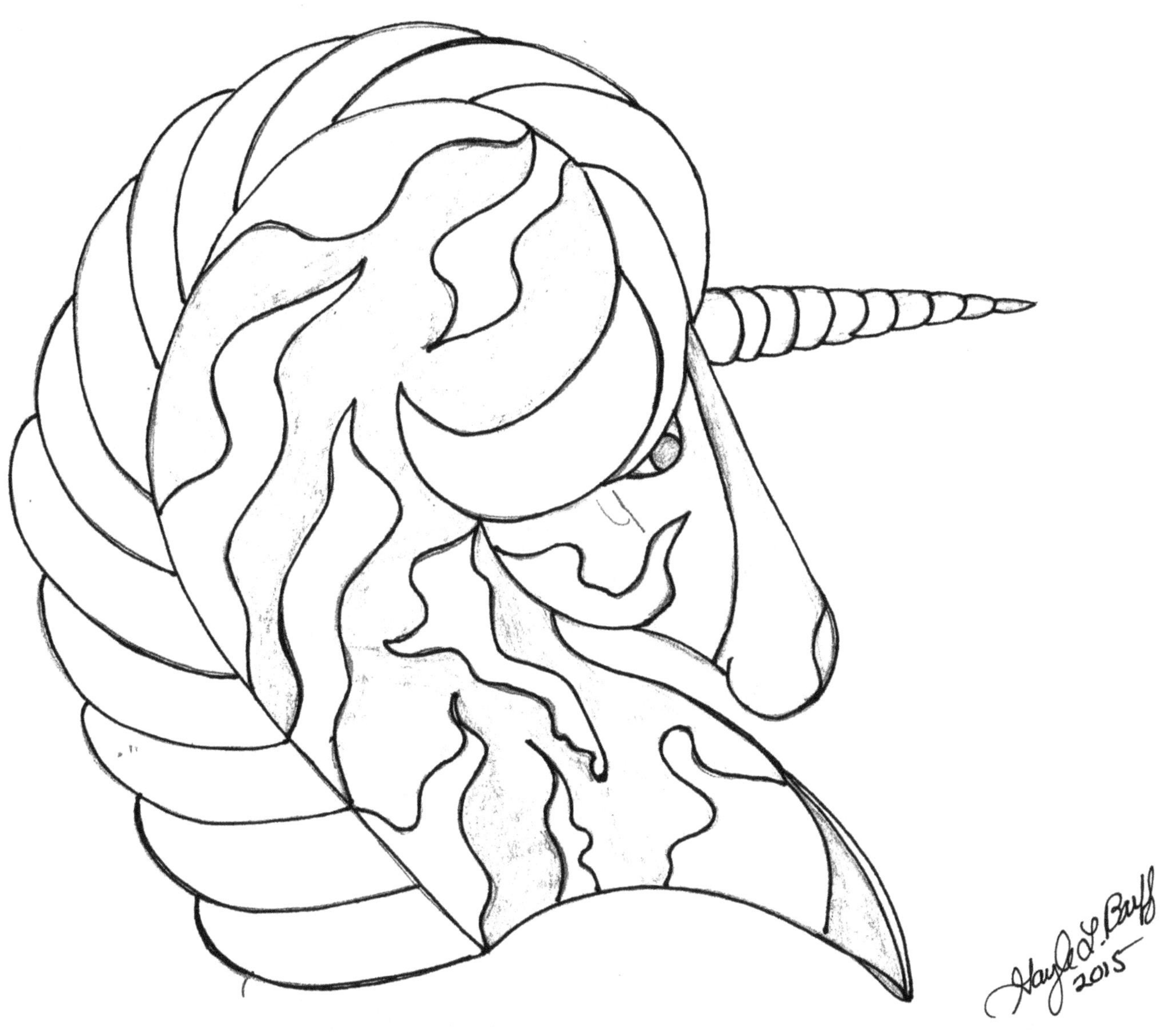

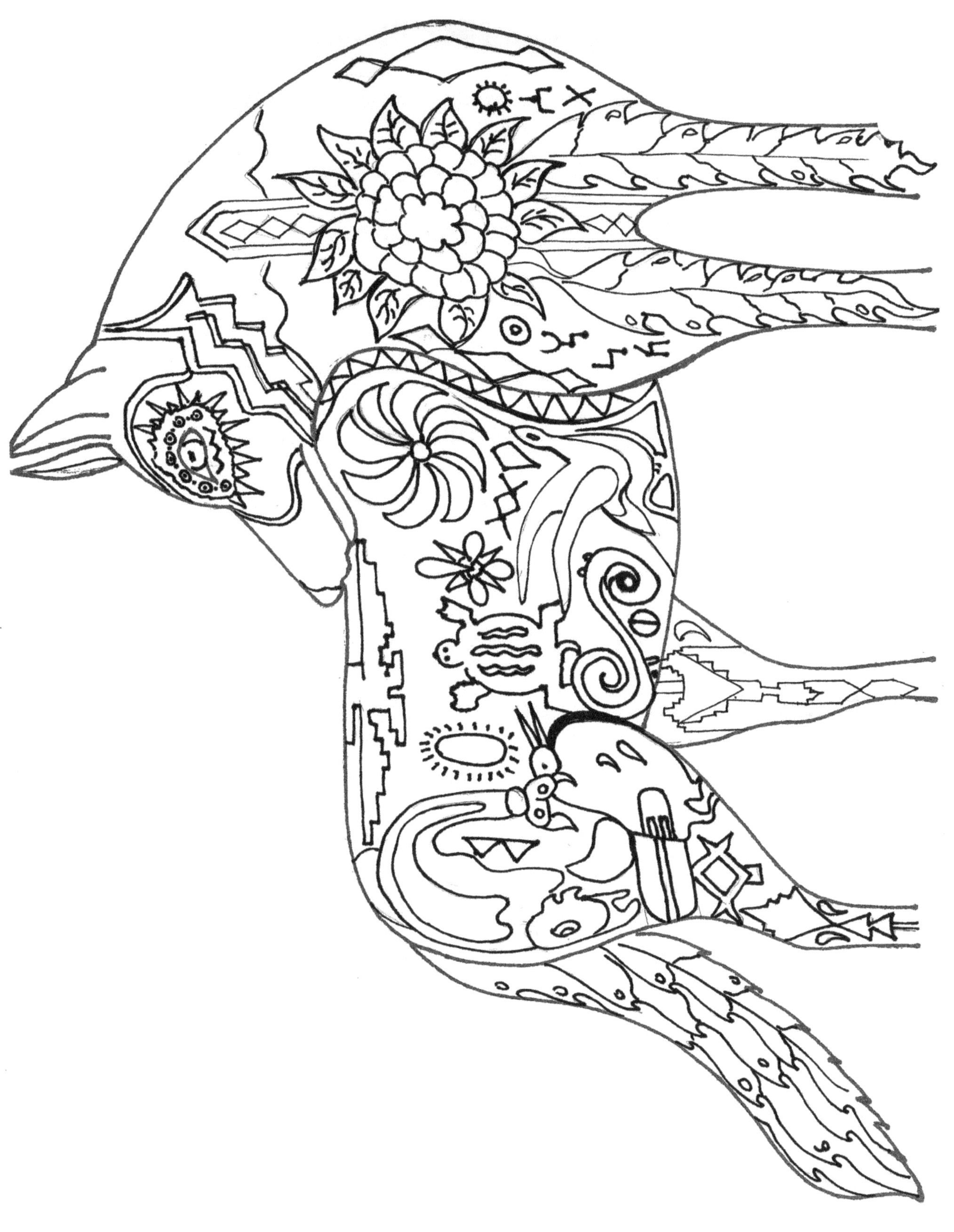

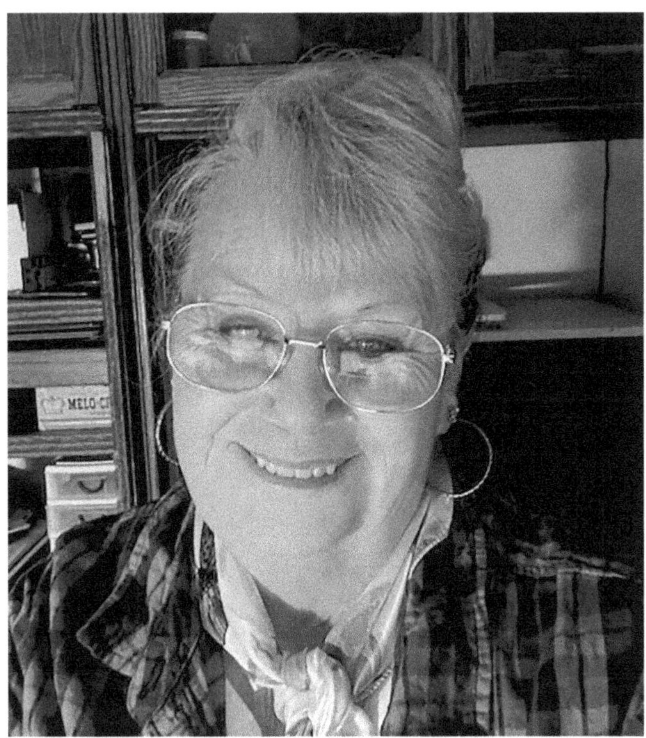

I was born and raised on the beautiful Mendocino Coast and spent my summers on our family ranch in Comptche, California. I went on to graduate from Mendocino Union High School and then spent some time in the San Francisco Bay area, where my daughter and son were born.

I enjoyed many years at Clearlake, California, where working nights allowed me to expand my artistic abilities, completely self-taught. I strongly believe that my Southwestern Indian Art comes from within; inspired by many ancestors that are traced back to the Cajun Choctaw Indians from Louisiana.

I come from a hard-working family of Loggers and Fishermen. My passions include my family, great friends, gardening, my home, my love for animals, and of course, my art. Now making my home with my husband, on a little farm on the Walker River, in Yerington, Nevada.

My art is changing and evolving every day; it has opened doors that I didn't know were there!

Sincerely,

Gayle L. Daufel

www.ingramcontent.com/pod-product-compliance
Lightning Source LLC
Chambersburg PA
CBHW041039050726
47599CB00018B/2014